BASIC TRAINING
FOR THE
PROPHETIC
MINISTRY

EXPANDED EDITION

DESTINY IMAGE BOOKS BY KRIS VALLOTTON

Developing a Supernatural Lifestyle

Supernatural Ways of Royalty

Basic Training for Prophetic Ministry

Basic Training for the Supernatural Ways of Royalty

KRIS VALLOTTON

BASIC TRAINING

FOR THE

PROPHETIC MINISTRY

EXPANDED EDITION

DESTINY IMAGE® PUBLISHERS, INC.
P.O. Box 310, Shippensburg, PA 17257-0310
"Promoting Inspired Lives."

Revised edition of Basic Training for the Prophetic Ministry by Destiny Image Publishers
Previous ISBN 10: 0-7684-2715-0
Previous ISBN 13 TP: 978-0-7684-2715-8

This book and all other Destiny Image and Destiny Image Fiction books are available at Christian bookstores and distributors worldwide.
For more information on foreign distributors, call 717-532-3040.
Reach us on the Internet: www.destinyimage.com.

ISBN 13 TP: 978-0-7684-0362-6
ISBN 13 Ebook: 978-0-7684-8492-2

For Worldwide Distribution, Printed in the U.S.A.
2 3 4 5 6 7 8 / 18 17 16 15

Contents

Foreword

ANEW GENERATION OF SOARING PROPHETIC EAGLES IS NOW HERE AMONG US. THESE risk-taking believers in the Lord Jesus Christ are not somewhere "out there" in the far distant future—they are with us now.

Kris Vallotton and his crew at Bethel Church's School of the Supernatural in Redding, California, seem to be leading the way! They have the highest level of impartation of any school of the supernatural that I know of anywhere today. Yes, that's right!

This generation of radical warriors is cut from a cloth different from my generation. We came from religion and learned the supernatural. But this generation is birthed in the supernatural and is soaring high in the things of God at an early age.

Wow—so where does that leave those in my generation? Are we left to be the bystanders just applauding the exploits of the new Joshua's and Caleb's? Absolutely not! There are new vistas for us each. In fact, I tell some of my students, "You are going to have to run fast to catch me 'cause I'm about to catch my second (or third) wind and I will outrun you all!" I think you get my drift.

Let me drive home my point by telling you one of my wife's many significant dreams. There was a line of men and women all standing neatly in a row—my wife, Michal Ann, was positioned there among them. An invitation was given by the Holy Spirit for fathers and mothers in the prophetic to step forward. In the dream, all of the others took a step backward so it appeared as though Michal Ann had just volunteered. Then a strong gust of wind hit her from behind and flung her even farther forward.

She was awakened out of the dream knowing somehow that she had just been chosen, or had volunteered with help, to be a mother of the prophetic in her generation. It was amazing to watch what the Lord did with this once withdrawn dear lady who had been thrust to the front of God's prophetic compassion army. If it could happen to Michal Ann and James W. Goll—it can happen to anyone! Remember—He is not a respecter of persons. He is looking for fresh volunteers at all times. There is room in His army for you!

That is what the manual you hold in your hands is about—Basic Training for the Prophetic Ministry. It is one of God's tools for this time and day, written from the trenches of great experience. My friend, Kris Vallotton, is one of the fathers in the making. Yes, there are many fathers and mothers who are volunteering to raise up the voice of the Lord.

Want to join them? Then tear apart this book. Lean in and learn all you can. Then take your hands out of your pockets, get your feet outside of the four walls of your church and home, open wide your mouth, and let the Holy Spirit fill it. Do something for Jesus' sake!

This manual is a call for passionate, consecrated warriors to arise. Therefore, it is with deep admiration and joy that I have the privilege of commending this training guide to you. Join Kris and I and a new-breed generation who are learning to fly high in the things of the Holy Spirit and take others with them. Volunteer freely in the day of His power and join His call to war!

Dr. James W. Goll
Cofounder of Encounters Network
Author of *The Seer, Dream Language,*
The Coming Prophetic Revolution, and many others
www.jamesgoll.com

Preface

For a long time, I taught the "How To's" of prophetic ministry: how to hear from the Lord, how to discern the different languages of God, and how to know *what* the prophetic is and what it is not. I spent a lot of time traveling the world, teaching people these key principles: what does the word "prophetic" actually mean, what is the difference between Old and New Testament prophecy, how do I receive the gift of prophecy, how do I articulate it, what is proper etiquette, how can I tell if I'm hearing from the right spirit, and so on.

After traveling and teaching these principles for about eight years, one day it dawned on me that I was teaching people how to *do* prophetic ministry, but I was not teaching them *why*. My first version of *Basic Training for the Prophetic* came out nearly ten years ago. This updated version is a blend of both the *why* and the *how to*.

As I started to think about the purpose of prophetic ministry, it struck me—prophecy is actually one of the love languages of God! I believe this message is for a new generation that God is raising up to bring His purposes to pass in the earth.

This manual is not necessarily for *the prophets*—people whose official position in the five-fold ministry is *prophet*. I believe these individuals will significantly benefit from this material, as it will practically help them to train others to have eyes and ears to hear God's voice. After all, that is one of our key functions as prophets. We cannot be the "go-to people" for believers to hear from God through. If anything, we train the Body of Christ how to hear from God for themselves.

The Bible identifies that while there is an official prophetic office, there is also a prophetic gifting available to all believers. So while we are going to cover the practical how-to's of prophetic ministry, I want to—up front—remind you of the purpose of the prophetic.

The prophetic is not about wowing people with a gifting, telling them their futures, or coming off as super-spiritual. It is not just about flowing in one of the gifts of the Spirit. God really wants to love people. This message is so urgently needed in our world of judgment, condemnation, fear, uncertainty, and anxiety. In an age when people are looking everywhere to discover a sense of acceptance and identity, *you* actually carry the solution to this crisis. His name is Holy Spirit, He lives inside you, and He wants to use you to be God's mouthpiece, telling the world that He really is *for* them, not against them.

You can see why it is very important to know the purpose of the prophetic before we start learning how to practice it. If, at the end of the day, we are fueled by a vision to see people connected with the love of God and His identity and destiny and purpose for their lives, we have truly grasped the "why" behind the prophetic ministry. Now, we are ready to step out and *be* the Father's mouthpiece to the world!

This manual was not written to be the final word on prophetic ministry. The goal was to help develop and facilitate prophetic communities. In addition to teaching how to minister prophetically, I also share a perspective that promotes a healthy community of believers. Therefore, I have intentionally emphasized instruction, which will assist leaders in shepherding the prophetic people of their communities.

With this in mind, there are thought-provoking questions and a Life Application section at the end of each chapter. The answers to the Questions to Ponder are found within the chapters. The Group Discussion Questions are not directly answered in the chapters, but are there to provoke thought and stimulate discussion. We often learn more through our own discovery than we do from someone else's teaching. These questions should help facilitate the discovery process.

The purpose of the Life Application section is to help you get past the obstacles that keep you from moving ahead in the prophetic ministry. There are also ideas about how to practically apply what you are learning.

Here are a few ways you can use this manual:

- Personal, individual study

- Small group study

- Church class study (Accompanying DVDs available)

My earnest prayer is that every Christian who reads this book will be drawn closer to God, and will join us in destroying the works of the devil.

Let the journey begin!

Introduction

IN THE DAYS OF THE PROPHET ELIJAH, THERE AROSE A COMPANY OF MEN WHO WERE called the *"sons of the prophets"* (1 Kings 20:35). These men traveled throughout the world ravaging the powers of darkness, wreaking havoc on evil kingdoms. They had no tolerance for the destructive behavior of wicked kings but rather turned many to righteousness. They raised the dead, healed the sick, parted rivers, destroyed false prophets, and saw revival spread throughout their land. They were feared by many and respected by all. They walked in great purity; and God was their friend.

Today, all around us, wickedness continues to grow, taking root in the lives of those we love and eroding the very foundation of our country. Satanism is spreading like wildfire. Psychics laugh in the face of the church as they demonstrate the power of the dark side. Divorce is destroying our families and violence is corrupting our children. Sickness and diseases take the lives of so many. Yet the words of our Lord Jesus echo through the halls of history, *"…he who believes in Me, the works that I do, he will do also; and greater works than these he will do; because I go to the Father"* (John 14:12).

In Acts 3:25, Peter says, *"It is you who are the sons of the prophets…."* It is time for the Body of Christ to rise up and receive our inheritance! We must rid ourselves of complacency and restore the ancient boundaries of holiness and demonstrations of great power. We cannot be satisfied with illustrative sermons, great music, and friendly services. We have been called to see the powers of darkness destroyed and our ruined cities restored.

In the days of Moses, God demonstrated His power to Pharaoh, but Pharaoh counter-attacked by having his sorcerers duplicate the miracles of God. Then the God of Heaven, who has all power, performed extraordinary miracles so that even the sorcerers said, "This must be God. We cannot perform these miracles." Finally Pharaoh was overcome by God's power and let His people go. (See Exodus 7-12.)

I believe that the Pharaoh of this age is about to let go of our cities as God demonstrates His raw power through His Church. We are in the midst of the greatest revival in human history. Yet there remains a distance between what should be and what will be.

That distance is you! What will you be?

You are the bridge between history and *His* story.

You are the sons of the prophets!

The sick, the demonized, the poor, the blind, the lame, and the lost are waiting to see what you have learned.

Don't disappoint them!

CHAPTER 1

The Purpose of Prophetic Ministry

This chapter explains how New Testament prophecy should function, explores the impact that prophecy has on people, and identifies the core values that should motivate prophetic ministry.

Prophetic Ministry—Looking for Treasure

Many of us are familiar with Jeremiah 29:11, where God tells His people, *"For I know the plans I have for you,' declares the Lord, 'plans to prosper you and not to harm you, plans to give you hope and a future'"* (New International Version).

Consider this. God made this statement to His people while they were in Babylonian captivity. They were in this place of bondage for 70 years because they had disobeyed God. Yet, we see the prophet Jeremiah speaking a very encouraging word, telling the people that God wanted to give them a future and a hope. Even though this seems to be contradictory—with God's people in Babylon because of their poor choices and disobedience, and God saying that He had plans to prosper them, giving them a hope and a future—we actually see a powerful picture of what the prophetic does.

Even though the people were in captivity, God spoke to their potential, not their present circumstance. In the same way, God uses the prophetic ministry today to address people's potential, not their present conditions. People sadly mistake the prophetic for the practice of calling out someone's sins, or unearthing their deep, hidden, sinful desires. Remember, God wants to communicate love and identity to people. As He spoke to His people in Babylonian captivity, He was not addressing their obvious circumstance. He was mining for the treasure He knew was in His people. God knows that if His word connects with the potential and destiny inside a person, a major shift begins to take place. Why? That person no longer sees him or herself as enslaved to the present identity or circumstances—rather, the prophetic introduces new options straight from Heaven.

The prophetic speaks to the value of people. The prophetic word, delivered by Jeremiah, reminded God's people that, even though they were in captivity, they were still valuable to God. This is the true *why* of the prophetic and it must motivate everything we do in the name of prophetic ministry.

The price that Jesus paid on the Cross determined the value of the people He purchased. God saw something good in us even when we were sinners (see Rom. 5:8). I like the way John and Carol Arnott say it, "Jesus didn't die for junk." Jesus made it very clear that *you* are a treasure in the field.

> **The price that Jesus paid on the Cross determined the value of the people He purchased.**

Jesus purchased the *whole* field. This included all the dirt, for the dirt was completely worth what was also present in the field: *you*. You are a treasure to God. People are treasures to God. This is why He was willing to make the ultimate exchange through the Cross. Again, what God gave in exchange for you and I—*His very Son*—reveals the incredible value that He places on humanity.

It doesn't take a prophetic gift to see the sin in sinners or the junk in the lives of Christians. It does require the eyes of God, though, to see broken people like Simon (Simon means "broken reed") and in the midst of their brokenness, call them Peter (Peter means "rock"). True prophetic ministry is looking for gold in the midst of the dirt in people's lives.

This is not simply patting people on the back, telling them nice things about themselves, and pretending away all of the negative, hoping it just resolves itself. The power of the prophetic is that it is supernatural encouragement. It does not offer flattering words, but when exercised properly, it actually hones in on the gold in people's lives and calls it out of them. It speaks to that gold, to that pearl, to that precious jewel in the midst of all the dirt, imperfection, confusion, guilt, shame, and sin.

> **True prophetic ministry is looking for gold in the midst of the dirt in people's lives.**

People know they are sinful. They are well aware that they make mistakes, fail, mess up again, fail some more, and seem to be incapable of getting on the right track. They deal with guilt, shame, and regret. What they do not know is that they are valuable to God. The prophetic actually awakens this reality in their lives and starts a process where people, previously blinded by their dirt and sin, start to rethink how they are living. After all, someone just gave them a new option. This is what the prophetic does. It confronts false mindsets and sinful thought patterns with new options.

Mere words of encouragement may bring a moment of relief or some form of flattery, but a prophetic word that speaks to the gold in people's life can actually be a catalyst that causes them to rethink life entirely. Why? Because no one had ever said *that* to them before, and maybe, *that* word is what their lifestyle should be reflecting rather than their present conditions.

From What Covenant Are You Prophesying?

"You have heard that it was said, 'You shall love your neighbor and hate your enemy.' But I say to you, love your enemies, bless those who curse you, do good to those who hate you, and pray for those who spitefully use you and persecute you. that you may be sons of your Father in heaven; for He makes His sun rise on the evil and on the good, and sends rain on the just and on the unjust" (Matthew 5:43-45 NKJV).

Unfortunately, there are believers, living under a New Testament blueprint, who are trying to prophesy as if they are still under the Old Testament system. To be like our Father in Heaven, we need to love our neighbor. This was a complete paradigm adjustment for those listening to Jesus; for up until He came on the scene, all they knew was the previous, "eye for an eye" system.

Think about the setting for a minute. The whole part about "Love your neighbor and hate your enemy" came from God. Under the Old Covenant, the same God actually sent the children of Israel into the Promised Land and commanded Joshua to kill everybody—the genocide of Gentiles. In the Old Covenant, your love for God was measured by your hatred for those who hated God. Even some of the familiar stories we tell in Sunday school, at their core, reflect this hatred toward the enemies of God. Why did David kill Goliath? Because the Philistines were enemies of God. It reads like a good story until you consider what David was doing—killing people who didn't love God. Goliath and the Philistines were the bad guys because they didn't love God. In fact, Israel's first king, Saul, was removed from his kingship because he extended mercy to a king who was condemned to death. Sometimes we try to skip over these details, but I believe it is very important for us to deal with them in a healthy way in order to make a proper comparison of Old and New Covenant realities.

How you understand the New Covenant will determine your concept of New Testament prophecy. The Old Covenant taught, "love your neighbor, hate your enemy." On the other hand, the New Testament mandate is to love everybody, even the people who don't love you and who don't love God.

Remember, the prophetic communicates the love of God to people. If we are prophesying out of an Old Covenant perspective, we are going to release words of condemnation and judgment. Old Covenant prophets judged cities and nations. This was the prophetic mandate under the previous system. The moral of the Old Testament was that you can't be good enough to get into Heaven and work for God's acceptance. You *need* a Savior. This is why everything we see under the Old Covenant is often so severe. The severity of the law confronts us with the severity of sin, and again, how desperate humankind needed a Savior. Sin so severe deserves judgment, hence why the prophetic voices under the Old Testament often released words of judgment. Time after time, the people of God were reminded through the prophets of God that they were in dire need of a Savior.

This was the Old Covenant. Now, we have a Savior. Everything has shifted. Jesus came and fulfilled the words of the Law and the prophets (see Matt. 5:17). Here is where we see the contrast between the two Testaments and how they give us different definitions of the prophetic. The goal of New Testament prophecy is that we would find treasure in the dirt of people's lives. Jesus bore our sins. He carried our shame. He was condemned so we would never have to be. Even though the Old Testament prophets released words of warning and judgment over the people, the people never were quite able to be obedient and follow instructions. Things have changed now; and as a result, how we approach prophetic ministry is very different under the New Covenant.

As we prophesy out of the New Covenant reality we have been redeemed to walk in, we will speak to the gold in a person and call it forth. New Testament prophecy is about finding the treasure in the dirt.

Finding Treasure in the Lives of Sinners

Paul tells us in First Corinthians that prophecy reveals the secrets of unbelievers' hearts.

> *But if all prophesy, and an unbeliever or an ungifted man enters, he is convicted by all, he is called to account by all; the secrets of his heart are disclosed; and so he will fall on his face and worship God, declaring that God is certainly among you* (1 Corinthians 14:24-25).

Notice in the passage that the person who receives the prophetic word doesn't repent but rather *"will fall on his face and worship God."* Most people know what is wrong with them but they are unaware of the greatness that God has placed in their lives. This is what prophecy identifies and calls out! Remember that Jesus didn't just die for our sins to be forgiven, but He offered up His life because we "fell short of the glory of God" (see Rom. 3:23). Prophecy brings people into a revelation of the glory that God has assigned to them. God's glory is the place that every person on the planet was created to live in, and live from. Jesus died for your sins *so* you could actually step into this revelation of glory. It is your inheritance—and the inheritance of every man, woman, and child in the world. Too many times, people mistakenly think that the more they go on and on about the sin and junk in someone's life, the more inclined that "sinner" will be to repent and turn to God. This is just not true. Paul tells us that it is the *goodness of God* that leads people to repentance (see Rom. 2:4). This foundation of God's goodness should also be the foundation for prophetic ministry. Instead of calling out people's sins, we should tell them about the glory God has intended for them to live in. Result? This exposure brings conviction in their lives that they are living below the glorious standard that God has set for them.

Returning to First Corinthians 14:25, we read that prophecy discloses the *"secrets of his heart"* (*"his"* refers to the "unbeliever" in this text). If we are prophesying out of an Old

Covenant perspective, we tend to look for negative or bad secrets to call out. That is not what Paul is talking about, for the context of prophecy is one of *"edification and exhortation and consolation"* (1 Cor. 14:3). Edification means to build up. Exhortation means to call near. Consolation means to comfort. These are three biblical criteria for how the prophetic ministry should operate and what kind of results it should produce in the people we are prophesying over. As a result of calling out secrets, people should not want to run and hide from us, fearing that we are messengers of God's wrath and judgment. Instead, the following is the desired result of the true prophetic in action: *"he will fall on his face and worship God, declaring that God is certainly among you"* (1 Cor. 14:25). Calling out the dirt only releases condemnation, shame, and judgment, while revealing secret treasures invites people to reconsider the road they are on in life and come face to face with their identity in Christ.

Most likely, the man Paul describes in First Corinthians 14:25 fell on his face and worshipped God, not because someone called out the dirt and sin in his life. He probably walked into a meeting, and someone there saw the treasure within him—the glory he fell short of—and showed him this treasure by delivering a prophetic word. Our goal is not to convict people of their sins. This is the Holy Spirit's job. Our role is to convict the world of the glory they fell short of. Through prophetic ministry, we remind the fallen world of the glory, beauty, and divine purpose it was meant to carry. Remember, sin is no secret to sinners—destiny is. Purpose is. Identity is. Unconditional love is. Gifts and callings are.

Prophecy reveals the secrets in unbelievers' hearts.

Prophetic Ministry Can Reconcile People to God

Therefore, if anyone is in Christ, he is a new creation; old things have passed away; behold, all things have become new. Now all things are of God, who has reconciled us to Himself through Jesus Christ, and has given us the ministry of reconciliation, that is, that God was in Christ reconciling the world to Himself, not imputing their trespasses to them, and has committed to us the word of reconciliation (2 Corinthians 5:17-19 NKJV).

The prophetic empowers you to participate in the ministry of reconciliation that has been assigned to all disciples of Christ. You are a new creation, a new creature, and a new species.

The word "new" actually means *prototype*. You are the first creature to ever live simultaneously in two dimensions. Apostle Paul writes about this in Ephesians 2:6, describing how we *"sit together in the heavenly places in Christ Jesus"* (NKJV). You live on earth and in Heaven at the same time. You have been given a completely new nature. You are not just a new spirit, but you are a whole new kind of creation. This is the place you prophesy from because, ultimately, this is the reality God is calling everyone to. The Father's heart is to reconcile all humankind to Himself. People, communities, and entire nations—His objective is reconciliation. This is the mission that the prophetic speaks to.

Again, it does not take prophetic insight to call someone out as being "distant from God" or "godless," particularly if they are not even a believer! But when you speak from a place, knowing that it is the Father's will and desire to bring this person into reconciliation with Him, you get to play a part in this supernatural ministry of reconciliation.

The key to following this example of the reconciling heart of God is found in Second Corinthians 5:19. The ministry of reconciliation involves *"not counting people's sins against them"* (New International Version). Every kind of ministry that we participate in, whether it is the ministry of helps, administration, healing, prophetic ministry, all of it is motivated by one central core—reconciliation. It is all about uniting humanity and God. If you step outside the ministry of reconciliation, there is a strong likelihood that you are carrying the wrong values in your ministry. Remember, a very specific ministry has been entrusted to us. Not one of condemnation. Not one of being in the spotlight. Not one of judgment. Not one of personal kingdom building. The ministry we have been given is the same ministry that Jesus had while He walked the earth. He was on a mission to reconcile humankind back to the Father, for even He did not count the world's sins against them (see John 3:16-17). He is our ultimate model.

Here is the tension you will deal with being one who prophesies out of a New Covenant heart and being motivated by the ministry of reconciliation—believers will often challenge your position. People will tell you, "Hollywood deserves to be judged for pornography and immorality." That is true. They will point to different cities or countries known for their immoral activity and claim that such people groups need to be judged because of their sin. While this is all true, that they deserve judgment for their sin, the troubling part is the standard we are holding up against these people. There is no question that sin deserves to be judged, and the Bible makes it very clear that there is a Day of Judgment coming. What amazes me is that, even though we all get into the Kingdom through Jesus' work, we want everybody else to get in through their works. This is why blatant sinful behavior makes so many people uncomfortable. While we cannot participate in it, we have not been called to judge it; we have been called to be ambassadors of reconciliation to those trapped in lifestyles of sin and tell them about the One whose work made it possible for them to become reunited with the Father.

It often does not begin with such a clear-cut presentation of the Gospel. This is why the prophetic ministry is so important, and why it is absolutely essential that we do not approach people according to their sins, but rather, according to the Father's will and desire, and that is for them to be reconciled. We speak to that. We prophesy to that potential.

Last Days' Prophetic Ministry

"And it shall be in the last days," God says, "that I will pour forth of My Spirit on all mankind; and your sons and your daughters shall prophesy..." (Acts 2:17).

The last days began on the Day of Pentecost and have been continuing ever since. For us to prophesy out of the right spirit, we must recognize the difference between the *last days* (plural) and *last day* (singular). Even though the difference seems pretty small, I can promise you, it makes all the difference in the world in how we approach prophetic ministry.

In Peter's sermon on Pentecost, he quotes the Old Testament prophet Joel who directly connects the last days outpouring of the Holy Spirit with sons and daughters prophesying. The prophetic obviously plays a key role in last days' ministry. So this naturally begs the questions, what is last days' ministry and how does it function?

This is why it is important to note the difference between the last days, as mentioned in the first part of the Acts passage, and the *great and glorious day of the Lord* that we see later on in verse 20.

"...and your young men shall see visions, and your old men shall dream dreams; even on My bondslaves, both men and women, I will in those days pour forth of My Spirit and they shall prophesy. And I will grant wonders in the sky above and signs on the earth below, blood, and fire, and vapor of smoke. The sun will be turned

into darkness and the moon into blood, before the great and glorious day of the Lord shall come. And it shall be that everyone who calls on the name of the Lord will be saved" (Acts 2:17-21).

We are not living in the great and terrible day of the Lord that verse 20 describes. This is the Day of Judgment. Nine times in the New Testament alone do we read about Judgment Day and it is often referred to as "great and terrible." Some passages that specifically address this single Day of Judgment are Acts 17:31, Second Peter 3:7, Jude 6, First John 4:17, and First Corinthians 4:4-5. On this day, only One will do the judging and that is God. He is the only One able to fulfill the role as Judge. On that day, there will be no prophesying; only pronouncements of judgment. It is just as incorrect for us to completely disregard Judgment Day as it is for us to prophesy judgment during the last days. Some have been going down this dangerous road, getting rid of Judgment Day all together, denying the reality of hell, and teaching that in the end, everyone makes it to Heaven. To believe this means you have to erase entire sections of Scripture, and basically rewrite the Bible.

The prophetic was not intended for the *Day*, as it will be no good at that point. Instead, we see that according to Joel's prophecy, the prophetic comes with the last *days*. In the same way the Pharisees missed Jesus because of their eschatology (understanding of the end times), many believers are missing their assignment in these last days because they are convinced that the last days is a summons for us to render judgment like God will on the last day. It is easy to get really harsh on the Pharisees, but the truth is, they had the Old Testament. They had access to the Scriptures. They were the pastors and teachers of their day. The problem is, they did not know what day it was; and when we don't know what day it is, we will not be able to prophesy accordingly.

Ultimately, if we believe that we are living in the Day of Judgment, we will pull prophetic judgments into this time period, when in fact, judgment is not reserved for our era. Judgment will be rendered on the last day, and God will be the only Judge. We have no place or authority to judge people, cities, or nations. Many believers are pronouncing judgment on the same type of people Jesus liked and hung out with. He struggled with religious people, but he really liked sinners. In fact, Jesus was always protecting sinners from the religious people. His strongest judgments were against the people who were supposed to know God, but didn't. On the other hand, He was very gracious with the people who didn't know God and didn't claim to. These are the people who some prophets like to judge; and I propose to you, based on what we have seen in the difference between the *last days* and the *last day*, that these are the people we have been called to reconcile to the Father.

Prophetic Ministry Can Change People's Hearts

In the ninth chapter of First Samuel there is a stirring story of prophetic ministry redirecting someone's heart.

Samuel answered Saul and said, "I am the seer. Go up before me to the high place, for you shall eat with me today; and in the morning I will let you go, and will tell you all that is on your mind. As for your donkeys which were lost three days ago, do not set your mind on them, for they have been found And for whom is all that is desirable in Israel? Is it not for you and for all your father's household?" Saul replied, "Am I not a Benjamite, of the smallest of the tribes of Israel, and my family the least of all the families of the tribe of Benjamin? Why then do you speak to me in this way?" Then Samuel took Saul and his servant and brought them into the hall and gave them a place at the head of those who were invited, who were about thirty men (1 Samuel 9:19-22).

Saul has been sent by his father to find their lost donkeys. After an unsuccessful venture, they decide to go to the nearest city to ask direction from a certain prophet. Meanwhile, God tells Samuel that Saul is coming to him to find his donkeys, and amazingly, he is to anoint him king of Israel. When Saul finally encounters Samuel, the prophet informs him that his donkeys are already found. Then he stuns Saul by asking him to stay until the next day in order to tell him all that is in his mind because he is the man in whom all the desires of Israel lie (see 1 Sam. 9:19). Saul is shocked and says to Samuel, *"Am I not a Benjamite, of the smallest of the tribes of Israel, and my family the least of all the families of the tribe of Benjamin? Why then do you speak to me in this way?"* (1 Sam. 9:21). Low self-esteem has caused many people to lose sight of the greatness that God has placed in them.

Notice in verse 19 that Samuel says he is going to tell him what is already in his mind (literally, heart). The story goes on to describe how Samuel anoints Saul king and tells him that he is going to encounter a group of prophets coming down from the hills.

Afterward you will come to the hill of God where the Philistine garrison is; and it shall be as soon as you have come there to the city, that you will meet a group of prophets coming down from the high place with harp, tambourine, flute, and a lyre before them, and they will be prophesying. Then the Spirit of the Lord will come upon you mightily, and you shall prophesy with them and be changed into another man (1 Samuel 10:5-6).

Let's break the story down. The first thing that happened, Saul received a prophetic word saying that he was going to be king of Israel. This was truly a secret buried deep in Saul's heart. This is exactly what Paul was talking about in First Corinthians 14, how calling out the secrets in one's heart is the true prophetic in action. The prophet Samuel was digging for buried treasure in Saul, who was suffering from low self-esteem. He considered himself among the smallest and the least, when in fact, God was speaking to him in a different way. This leads right into the second point.

The next morning, Samuel anoints Saul king of Israel. It is interesting to note that, based on what we read in First Samuel 10:6, Saul was not transformed into a "different" man, but instead, the verse reads *"another man."* Samuel told Saul what was *already* in his heart. Saul did not morph into a completely different person; but rather, he came into alignment with the potential and identity that he was originally created for. This is what New Testament prophetic ministry is purposed to do—call out the treasure in spite of the issues, in spite of the self-esteem problems, in spite of the sin, in spite of the mistakes and bad choices. However, Saul needed a new heart in order to embrace his original design.

Then it happened when he turned his back to leave Samuel, God changed his heart; and all those signs came about on that day. When they came to the hill there, behold, a group of prophets met him; and the Spirit of God came upon him mightily, so that he prophesied among them (1 Samuel 10:9-10).

This is an Old Testament picture of the miraculous work that God performs on us through the Holy Spirit. For those who have not yet received salvation and have not entered into the Kingdom, there is still destiny on them. There is purpose, calling, and God-assigned identity. In fact, we are called to prophesy to those who are in the pre-Christian stage because as we prophesy over them, they see glimpses of who they have been created to be.

To step into this identity, the Spirit of God causes them to recognize that they need a new heart in order to embrace their original design. This often becomes a powerful setup for salvation. It may or may not happen instantly; that is not your job. Your job is to call out the secret treasure in their hearts, reminding them, like Samuel did to Saul, of everything that is already inside of their hearts that they are currently unable to see. However, you *can* see it because the Spirit of God is in you.

By the time Saul turned to leave, he was changed into another man. He was transformed into the man who he was designed to be from the beginning. The real man who was hidden under low self-esteem and sin was revealed and restored. This is the heart of true prophetic ministry!

Does Greatness Promote Pride?

Some believe that calling out greatness in people promotes pride. True humility is not thinking less of yourself but thinking of yourself less. The truth of God's grace humbles people without degrading them and exalts people without inflating them.

"Prophecy calls out the greatness in people."

Some time ago I was teaching on the purposes of prophetic ministry. Beginning with a few opening comments, I said, "Prophecy calls out the greatness in people."

Just then a pastor walked through the back door and said, "I have a question."

"What is it?"

"I believe that God is great," he said.

"Yes. Did I say something that made you feel that God wasn't great?"

"You said we are to call out the greatness in people. I believe that you are creating pride in people by doing that," he said.

I fired back, "I believe that for years the church has emasculated and castrated people in the name of humility." I pointed to a beautiful painting on the wall and said, "Let's pretend you painted that picture."

"OK," he said, looking confused.

"That's a stupid looking painting! Look at those ugly colors!" I yelled. "Now," I asked him, "Did demeaning the painting glorify the artist?"

"No," he said.

"Isn't it true that the beauty of the painting actually brings honor to the artist?"

"Yes, that's true," he said.

"You didn't paint yourself—God painted you," I told him. "Not only that, but Jesus is the One who sat in the chair and modeled for the portrait. We are created in His image and in His likeness. Every time we demean ourselves we are talking badly about the Artist and the Model. The truth is that the beauty of creation actually gives glory to the Creator."

True Humility Expressed

There is an interesting story in Daniel chapter 4. Nebuchadnezzar has a dream about a large, beautiful tree being cut down by an angel. Daniel interprets the dream to mean that "Nebs" is about to lose his mind for seven years because of his arrogance and pride. He will become like an animal until he recognizes that God is the ruler of the world. Twelve months later, the king is on the roof of his castle telling himself how awesome he is for having built Babylon with his own strength and power.

Just then he goes insane. He becomes like an animal, living in the fields eating grass. After seven years, his sanity returns. Look at the first words Nebuchadnezzar says when he could finally speak instead of mumble:

> *At that time my reason returned to me and my majesty and splendor were restored to me for the glory of my kingdom, and my counselors and my nobles began seeking me out; so I was reestablished in my sovereignty, and surpassing greatness was added to me. Now I, Nebuchadnezzar, praise, exalt and honor the King of heaven, for all His works are true and His ways just, and He is able to humble those who walk in pride* (Daniel 4:36-37).

Nebuchadnezzar is saying, "I am humbly awesome!" Humility is not demeaning yourself, it is exalting our God!

Questions to Ponder

1. What is the main purpose for prophetic ministry?

   _____

   _____

2. What did we fall short of when we were sinners?

   _____

   _____

3. What are the secrets of people's hearts?

   _____

   _____

4. What is the difference between the "last days" and "the last day" and how does understanding this impact the way we operate in prophetic ministry?

   _____

   _____

   _____

   _____

5. What is true humility?

   _____

   _____

   _____

   _____

6. Who were you modeled after when you were created?

   _____

   _____

Questions for Group Discussion

1. What is the difference between Old and New Testament prophecy?

2. Explain how New Testament prophecy operates. What is the goal?

3. How can I be involved with sinful people and still call out the greatness in them?

4. Is there a time when it is wrong to show people the glory that God has hidden in them?

Life Application

Think of one person in your life with whom you have the most problems. Spend some time praying for that person. Ask the Holy Spirit to reveal to you one aspect of the glory of God that is assigned to that person. Now, go tell that person what you see and observe how this affects your relationship.

CHAPTER 2

Prophets and Prophecy

Have you ever wondered what the difference is between the Gift of Prophecy and the Office of Prophet? In this chapter the many mysteries that have baffled the church for generations are unraveled.

Understanding the Spirit Realm

The gift of prophecy is one of the nine manifestation gifts of the Holy Spirit listed in First Corinthians 12. Before we understand the gift of prophecy, and what differentiates it from the office of a prophet, it is important that we clearly grasp what Paul is trying to tell us in the following verses. To operate in any gift of the Holy Spirit demands a correct understanding of the spirit realm—a subject that many prefer to run from in fear and mystery rather than run toward in faith and clarity.

Paul writes to the church in Corinth:

> *Now concerning spiritual gifts, brethren, I do not want you to be unaware. You know that when you were pagans, you were led astray to the mute idols, however you were led. Therefore I make known to you that no one speaking by the Spirit of God says, "Jesus is accursed"; and no one can say, "Jesus is Lord," except by the Holy Spirit* (1 Corinthians 12:1-3).

In your Bible, there is a good chance that the word "gifts" is italicized. The reason *gifts* is italicized is because it is not present in the original Greek language. It is a mistake in the translation.

If you read the English Standard Version, it gives a little more clarity. Beside the word *gifts* is a note indicating that the phrase *spiritual gifts* could be exchanged for *"spiritual persons."* Perhaps the most accurate translation would be Young's Literal Translation, which phrases verse 1 this way: *"And concerning the spiritual things, brethren, I do not wish you to be ignorant...."*

This is how it reads in the original Greek: *"Now concerning the spiritual, brethren, I don't want you to be unaware."*

How we understand this verse, in its proper context, makes all the difference when approaching the subject of spiritual gifts—including the specific gift of prophecy. Let us explore a few things that Paul was doing when trying to correct the Corinthians' understanding of the spirit realm.

First, and most foundationally, Paul was providing a correct understanding of the spirit realm to a people who were previously involved in paganism and polytheism. It is important to know who Paul's context was. We see this in verse 2, as he writes, *"You know that when you were pagans, you were led astray to the mute idols, however you were led."* The Corinthians were pagan, idol-worshipping, polytheists (recognized multiple gods). They worshipped many gods before they came to Christ. It would make sense, then, that Paul would want to retrain the way they understood the spirit realm. After all, coming from a world of paganism, the Corinthians did have a concept of the spirit realm—unfortunately, it was off.

Second, Paul was helping people—who previously worshipped many gods—understand how one God could move in multiple ways. Pay attention to how Paul goes on to list the gifts of the Holy Spirit and some of the repeat language he uses in describing their operation.

Now there are varieties of gifts, but the same Spirit. And there are varieties of ministries, and the same Lord. There are varieties of effects, but the same God who works all things in all persons. But to each one is given the manifestation of the Spirit for the common good. For to one is given the word of wisdom through the Spirit, and to another the word of knowledge according to the same Spirit; to another faith by the same Spirit, and to another gifts of healing by the one Spirit, and to another the effecting of miracles, and to another prophecy, and to another the distinguishing of spirits, to another various kinds of tongues, and to another

the interpretation of tongues. But one and the same Spirit works all these things, distributing to each one individually just as He wills (1 Corinthians 12:4-11).

What is the key active word in these verses? The word *same*. This word is key in giving his audience an appropriate introduction to the spirit realm. Remember, they worshipped many gods. Even as believers, the Corinthians had to experience a renewing of the mind. Old ideas about spirituality had to be replaced with the truth about who God was and how He operated. For them to recognize that it was the same Spirit who performed each of these nine supernatural exploits was a huge shift. Without this understanding, the Corinthians—most likely—thought that there was a god for each gift. When a healing happened, the healing god was at work. When a prophetic word went forth, the prophetic god was in operation. When miracles took place, the god of miracles was up to something.

Even though we could argue that the Corinthians were some of the most spiritual people, they were also some of the most ignorant concerning the truth of the spirit realm. Again, this is why Paul keeps repeating *the same Spirit* or *the same God*.

Paul is not so focused on the gifts of the Spirit as he is helping the Corinthians have a proper view of the spirit world and how it really works. These people were taught about Hercules and the different Greek gods. They were familiar with mythology, and that is from where they built their understanding of the spirit realm. Paul was basically saying, "That stuff is *not real;* let me explain to you who is real and how His realm operates."

The first group that needs to overcome its ignorance of the spirit world are the ones who came out of complete darkness and paganism. But there is another.

There are also people who try to make sense of spiritual gifts without first rightly understanding the spirit realm. While I propose there are far more than nine spiritual gifts, the key factor that makes a spiritual gift a *spiritual gift* is the supernatural element. The nine examples Paul lists in First Corinthians 12:4-11 remind us that a gift of the Holy Spirit is something that *He* gives supernaturally. They are not innate talents, although we are very grateful for these. They are not learned or acquired skills, although we can learn how to grow and develop in the gifts. The gifts of the Spirit are supernatural endowments of power given by the Holy Spirit, completely and totally by grace.

The spirit realm is more real than the natural realm. It actually pre-existed the natural. Before there was substance, there was the spirit realm, for everything that was made came out of God's realm.

Either way, if we want to learn how to operate in the prophetic, we must be willing to biblically grasp how the spirit realm works. This is the first step in understanding the gift of prophecy.

The Gift of Prophecy

The gift of prophecy is one of the nine manifestation gifts of the Holy Spirit listed in First Corinthians 12:4-11:

Now there are varieties of gifts, but the same Spirit. And there are varieties of ministries, and the same Lord. There are varieties of effects, but the same God who works all things in all persons. But to each one is given the manifestation of the Spirit for the common good. For to one is given the word of wisdom through the Spirit, and to another the word of knowledge according to the same Spirit; to another faith by the same Spirit, and to another gifts of healing by the one Spirit, and to another the effecting of miracles, and to another prophecy, and to another the distinguishing of spirits, to another various kinds of tongues, and to another the interpretation of tongues. But one and the same Spirit works all these things, distributing to each one individually just as He wills.

We are to earnestly desire spiritual gifts. Earnestly desire means to "lust after"—God wants us to pursue His gifts with passion and intensity! He desires to give us His gifts more than we could ever want them.

Pursue love, yet desire earnestly spiritual gifts, but especially that you may prophesy. For one who speaks in a tongue does not speak to men but to God; for no one understands, but in his spirit he speaks mysteries. But one who prophesies speaks to men for edification and exhortation and consolation (1 Corinthians 14:1-3).

Prophecy Is a Gift—Not an Award

As we discover what the *gift* of prophecy is, the first thing we must know is that we cannot earn it! We received it by asking. It is not an award or reward; the gift of prophecy is given, by grace, as a gift. We did not earn it. We could not work hard for it. We do not deserve it. The gifts of the Holy Spirit are supernatural endowments that you receive without merit or earning.

Two important things we must recognize about the gifts of the Spirit:

First, you can have all of the gifts because the Giver lives inside you. Some have taught that you are limited to one particular gift, and that is the only gift that the Holy Spirit will ever use in your life. This falls under what we looked at previously, where people start thinking of the gifts of the Spirit more like talents or innate abilities. Although it is true that some may gravitate toward certain gifts—such as those who move more in the gift of healing and others who move in the gift of prophecy—you have access to all of the gifts because the Holy Spirit lives inside you. He is the gift distributor.

First Corinthians 12:11 makes it clear that "*one and the same Spirit works all these things, distributing to each one individually just as He wills.*" The Holy Spirit decides who gets to operate in one or multiple gifts. The key is asking. This is how the Holy Spirit determines who He gives the gifts to. Asking is a main principle of the Kingdom, with Jesus saying, "*Ask, and it will be given to you; seek, and you will find; knock, and it will be opened to you*" (Matt. 7:7).

Second, this would imply that even very gifted people are not necessarily mature Christians. They may not even have good character. Therefore, it is important for us to recognize that the gifts of the Spirit do not validate our walk with God. They can never serve as the measuring stick for spiritual maturity. Rather, it is the fruit of the Spirit that is developed as a person matures in Christ. The Greek word for gift is *charis* or *charisma*, which means favor that one receives without any merit of his or her own. The fruit of the Spirit is the evidence of maturity in our lives. This fruit grows in our lives as we allow the Holy Spirit to work in us—not just through us.

But the fruit of the Spirit is love, joy, peace, patience, kindness, goodness, faithfulness, gentleness, self-control; against such things there is no law (Galatians 5:22-23).

The fruit of the Spirit is a sign that you actually have a relationship with God. Again, God is not just working through you, using the gifts of the Holy Spirit—He is actually working on you and you are embracing His growing work in your life.

When the Day of Judgment comes, there will be those who say, "*Lord, Lord, did we not prophesy in Your name, and in Your name cast out demons, and in Your name perform many miracles?*" (Matt. 7:22). Even though these people moved in power, they used the wrong measuring stick when standing before the Lord. It had nothing to do with what they did, but rather, who they were. They were basically saying, "God, I did these things for You...but I was not actually committed to You." This is why the Lord responds, "*I never knew you...*" in verse 23.

Even though we can demonstrate power without love, Jesus did not give you and me an example where this would need to be the case. It is not either/or—it is both. The same Holy Spirit who causes us to act more like Christ in our character enables us to act more like Him in power.

The Goal of Prophecy

But one who prophesies speaks to men for edification and exhortation and consolation (1 Corinthians 14:3).

The gift of prophecy is for the purpose of edification, exhortation, and consolation. Edification means "to build up." Exhortation means "to call near." Consolation means "to cheer up."

One exercise I recommend: before sharing a prophetic word with someone else, try it out on yourself. Then evaluate: How do I feel about that word? Does it feel like it would build that person up and edify him or her? Does it bring exhortation? Does it console?

The gift of prophecy—along with the other listed gifts of the Holy Spirit—are for edification. They are to build people up. In fact, they communicate the love language of God. When you prophesy over someone, does the person feel *kissed* by God? When someone moves in healing, the person they are ministering to should feel embraced by God. No one should have to be *delivered* from their last deliverance. Moving in the gifts of the Holy Spirit should not be likened to supernatural chemotherapy, where cells die in order to maintain life. Remember, the goal is to build up, call near, and cheer up!

To walk in Christian maturity, we should familiarize ourselves with the nine fruit of the Spirit, the nine gifts, and the nine Beatitudes listed by Jesus. If you want to live a well-balanced life, you will want to have the attitudes of the Spirit (Beatitudes), the fruit of the Spirit, and the gifts of the Spirit moving and operating through your life. Jesus never gave us a vision of Christianity where we got to pick and choose which ones we wanted, and which ones we could do without. Some mistakenly think that, since the fruit of the Spirit are the signs of our relationship with God and evidence of Christian maturity, they are the ones we should be exclusively going after at the expense of the gifts. This is not the case, as Paul gave us a very clear command in First Corinthians 14:1, *"Pursue love, yet desire earnestly spiritual gifts, but especially that you may prophesy."*

We are encouraged to desire the gifts so strongly because of the positive results they produce, in both the Body of Christ and upon those who have not even given their lives to Christ yet.

To Encourage the Church

The primary purpose of the gift of prophecy is not to direct or correct the Body of Christ, but rather to *encourage* the church. In Acts 15:32, we see Luke draw a direct comparison to prophets and the ministry of encouragement as he writes that *"Judas and Silas, also being prophets themselves, encouraged and strengthened the brethren."* New Testament prophecy encourages, not condemns or speaks negatively. We should never allow people who are ministering in the gift of prophecy to speak negatively into the lives of others. The goal of the gift of prophecy is to *bring out the best in people!* We are to mine the gold that is within the dirt and find hidden treasures in people's lives. If we see negative things in someone's life we are ministering to, we are to ask the Holy Spirit to give us the answer to the problem we discern. Then we prophesy the *answer*—not the problem.

We must declare and release the solutions, not the issues. That way, the person we are prophesying to will receive grace to solve the problem. When people speak negatively and condemningly over others, and then call it prophecy, all they have done is make them more aware of their problems or issues without giving them any type of supernatural solution on how to solve it. It just leaves them hanging—and feeling badly about it!

For example, if we are ministering to someone and discern that they are struggling with pornography, the Holy Spirit will often give us a prophetic word for them such as: "God is calling you to a new level of purity and holiness." In this way, we have prophesied the answer without speaking about the problem and have released grace to break the bondage of pornography.

Prophecy encourages the Church.

Anyone who is saved and receives the baptism of the Holy Spirit can minister in the gifts of the Spirit. However, it is important for us to examine the difference between the gift of prophecy and the office of the *prophet*.

 *For you can all prophesy one by one, so that all may learn and all may be exhorted* (1 Corinthians 14:31).

"And it shall be in the last days," God says, "That I will pour forth of My Spirit on all mankind; and your sons and your daughters shall prophesy, and your young men shall see visions, and your old men shall dream dreams; even on My bondslaves, both men and women, I will in those days pour forth of My Spirit and they shall prophesy" (Acts 2:17-18).

The Difference between Prophets and the Gift of Prophecy

Christ gave the prophets to the Church as a gift. We see this in Ephesians 4:7-13, as the apostle Paul discusses the five-fold ministry offices. He specifically calls these offices—apostle, prophet, evangelist, teacher, and pastor—gifts to the Body of Christ, for *"the equipping of the saints for the work of service, to the building up of the body of Christ"* (v. 12). The main function of a prophet is to equip the saints to do the work of service. The prophet equips the Church with eyes to see and ears to hear.

The prophet can never substitute our need to hear from God for ourselves, nor does our need to hear God for ourselves replace the need for the prophets. The prophetic office is not about building one person up as *the person* who hears from God for everyone else. Prophets are given to the Body of Christ to help each one of us hear God for ourselves all the more clearly. The prophet's job is to work him or herself out of a job. If we are in a culture where we always need a prophetic word, and we are constantly going to a prophet to receive advice, discernment, direction, clarity, and a sense of God's voice, we are functioning in an immature culture. In this environment, someone is clearly misrepresenting the office of a prophet since the prophet's primary job is to give *the Body of Christ* eyes to see and ears to hear God for themselves.

The grace that prophets carry can cause people to be able to hear the voice of the Spirit. Prophets have the authority to correct and direct because they are part of the government of God.

The Calling of a Prophet or Prophetess

The office of the prophet is a life calling. Most prophets are called at birth or when they are born again. I do not believe that this is something you ask for or seek to become. You cannot go to school to become a prophet or receive some type of diploma certifying that you are a prophet. It is the Lord's choosing, as are all of the five-fold ministry gifts of Ephesians 4. However, if you are called, you still have the responsibility to develop your gift. I remember hearing Graham Cooke say many years ago during a conference, "It takes fourteen years for a person to develop into a prophet after being called."

But to each one of us grace was given according to the measure of Christ's gift. Therefore it says, "When He ascended on high, He led captive a host of captives, and He gave gifts to men." (Now this expression, "He ascended," what does it mean except that He also had descended into the lower parts of the earth? He who descended is Himself also He who ascended far above all the heavens, so that He might fill all things.) And He gave some as apostles, and some as prophets, and some as evangelists, and some as pastors and teachers, for the equipping of the saints for the work of service, to the building up of the body of Christ; until we all attain to the unity of the faith, and of the knowledge of the Son of God, to a mature man,

to the measure of the stature which belongs to the fullness of Christ (Ephesians 4:7-13).

In order for us to receive the grace that allows us to see and hear (which is the prophet's reward), we must receive the prophet in the name of a prophet.

He who receives a prophet in the name of a prophet shall receive a prophet's reward; and he who receives a righteous man in the name of a righteous man shall receive a righteous man's reward (Matthew 10:41).

Each of us receives from people based on the role that we understand them to play in our lives. For example, someone seeking counsel from a prophet must realize that, unlike a pastor (whose best counsel comes after much listening), a prophet will often give his or her best insight with little or no prior information. A person trying to receive this type of counsel without understanding the gift and role of the prophet may think to themselves, *How can you give me counsel when you don't even understand my situation?* Therefore, it is important for us to understand the various roles that the members of the Body of Christ play in our lives.

The Five-Fold Ministry

The following is a very brief overview of the governmental offices in the church. Included is a short description of their roles in the Body of Christ, giving understanding and assistance in receiving their ministry into our lives.

- Apostles govern. Apostles are similar to the general contractor who oversees the project and sees the overall picture.

- Prophets guide. Prophets are the architects who assist the general contractor to know what the project should look like.

- Evangelists gather. Evangelists' concern is for the lost.

- Pastors guard. A pastor's heart is for the saved.

- Teachers ground. A teacher's primary role is to help the flock understand the Word of God. Paul did not say, "I have the mind of Christ." He said, *"We have the mind of Christ"* (1 Cor. 2:16.) We gain the balance we need and God's perspective on situations when we learn to value the members of the Body who think differently from the way we do!

The Difference between Prophets and Prophecy

To be a prophet is a calling.

To minister in prophecy is a gift.

When a person ministers in the gift of prophecy, the gift is the ability to prophesy. The words themselves are the gift. When a person is a prophet, the person him or herself is the gift. The Book of Ephesians says, *"Christ gave gifts to men."* The gifts that Christ gave to men and women are other men and women. A prophet is a gift to the church.

There are actually three components to any mature ministry. These components include calling, gifting, and anointing—all important elements of fruitful ministry.

- Calling gives identity. *"Paul, called as an apostle of Jesus Christ by the will of God"* (1 Cor. 1:1).

- Gifting gives ability. *"As each one has received a special gift, employ it in serving one another as good stewards of the manifold grace of God"* (1 Pet. 4:10).

- Anointing gives purpose. *"The Spirit of the Lord God is upon me, because the Lord has anointed me to bring good news to the afflicted; He has sent me to bind up the brokenhearted, to proclaim liberty to captives and freedom to prisoners"* (Isa. 61:1).

The gifts and callings of God are irrevocable but the anointing of the Lord ebbs and flows according to the relationship we have with the Holy Spirit.

Therefore, we must realize that the calling on our lives describes who we are. The anointing of God provides us with our purpose in life. The gifts that God has given to us become the abilities through which we accomplish His purposes.

The gifts and the calling of God are irrevocable (Romans 11:29).

41

Prophecy Defined

Prophecy in the purest sense is foretelling and forthtelling.

Foretelling—to know the future.

The following is an example of foretelling. Agabus speaks prophetically about a famine that will take place worldwide. It happens a few years later.

One of them named Agabus stood up and began to indicate by the Spirit that there would certainly be a great famine all over the world. And this took place in the reign of Claudius (Acts 11:28).

Forthtelling—to cause the future.

A great example of forthtelling is in the following passages in Ezekiel. God instructs the prophet Ezekiel to prophesy to dead bones and they became a mighty army. Ezekiel just didn't tell the future, he caused the future!

The hand of the Lord was upon me, and He brought me out by the Spirit of the Lord and set me down in the middle of the valley; and it was full of bones. He caused me to pass among them round about, and behold, there were very many on the surface of the valley; and lo, they were very dry.

He said to me, "Son of man, can these bones live?" And I answered, "O Lord God, You know." Again He said to me, "Prophesy over these bones and say to them, 'O dry bones, hear the word of the Lord.' Thus says the Lord God to these bones, 'Behold, I will cause breath to enter you that you may come to life. I will put sinews on you, make flesh grow back on you, cover you with skin and put breath in you that you may come alive; and you will know that I am the Lord.'"

So I prophesied as I was commanded; and as I prophesied, there was a noise, and behold, a rattling ; and the bones came together, bone to its bone. And I looked, and behold, sinews were on them, and flesh grew and skin covered them; but there was no breath in them. Then He said to me, "Prophesy to the breath, prophesy, son of man, and say to the breath, 'Thus says the Lord God,

"Come from the four winds, O breath, and breathe on these slain, that they come to life."""

So I prophesied as He commanded me, and the breath came into them, and they came to life and stood on their feet, an exceedingly great army (Ezekiel 37:1-10).

Difference between Prophecy and the Word of Knowledge

People often confuse the word of knowledge with the gift of prophecy. The word of knowledge describes something that took place in the past, a current circumstance, or a fact about someone's life. Sometimes when we prophesy, someone can mistakenly think that the prophecy wasn't accurate because it is not something that is currently happening, or has ever happened in that person's life. Pure prophecy is about the future. If the prophetic word lacks an element of something that has already taken place, this simply means that the word of knowledge was not part of the delivery. A word of knowledge is simply knowing a fact, revealed by the Holy Spirit, of which we had no prior knowledge.

Levels of Prophecy

There are generally four levels of prophecy: prophetic culture; the gift of prophecy; prophetic people; and prophets and prophetesses.

Level 1—Prophetic Culture

A prophetic culture takes place when a prophet or high-level prophetic anointing is present in a geographic location—in this atmosphere, even non-prophetic people can prophesy, although they may never prophesy again. This is demonstrated in the life of King Saul. When he was pursuing David in the wilderness, he encountered a group of prophets who were prophesying in the desert. Suddenly, the Spirit of prophecy fell upon Saul and he prophesied along with the prophets even though he was wicked! The people asked, *"Is Saul among the prophets?"* (1 Sam. 19:24). People ministering on this level are actually operating out of someone else's anointing. You might say they are borrowing from someone else. In a prophetic atmosphere, even a donkey can speak for God! (See Numbers 22:28-30.)

Level 2—The Gift of Prophecy

This second level of prophecy has been discussed earlier in this chapter. It is simply the Holy Spirit's gifts working in and through a person. Most of the information in this book is dedicated to this level of prophecy.

Level 3—Prophetic People

These people are not prophets because that is not the call on their lives; but they operate in the gift of prophecy at a high level. They also have a proven prophetic ministry and they have a strong relationship with the church leadership. Therefore, they are often allowed to direct and perhaps even correct people within their local congregation. This type of trusted relationship can take years to develop.

Level 4—Prophets and Prophetesses

This is the highest level of prophetic ministry, which was mentioned previously.

The Three Parts of Prophecy

- Revelation: The person who gives the prophetic word is responsible for the revelation of the word. It may come as a dream, a vision, or any of the ways that are explained in the next chapter.

- Interpretation: What does the revelation mean? Prophetic people need to realize that just because they had the revelation does not mean that they also have the interpretation. We often get into trouble when we try to interpret a vision or some other form of God's voice without first receiving God's direction and clarity.

- Application: What should we do with the word once we know what it means? Our pastor or overseer should always be involved when the prophetic word includes direction. They should help the recipient of the word devise a plan to actually apply it to their life and walk it out.

The easiest way to summarize the three parts of prophecy: When God stops speaking, we should too! People who are prophesying often feel the pressure to give an interpretation, particularly when the prophetic word seems ambiguous or even silly. It is astounding what some people think their prophetic words mean! The following is a profound example of a powerful prophetic word that was misinterpreted by the person who delivered it. Remember, we don't have to be profound to be powerful.

Some time ago several of us traveled to a MorningStar conference where they were training people how to prophesy. With about 70 people in the room, we were all prophesying to a woman in the front of the room. When we had completed the ten prophecies allowed each person, and began to judge the words given, a man in the back of the room stood to his feet and said, "You have on a yellow shirt!"

Immediately the woman fell to the ground, crying hysterically. The man continued to prophesy, saying things like, "The sun is yellow...the moon is yellow," and so on. When the woman finally regained her composure, the leader of the class asked her what that word meant to her.

She explained, "I have a son who is autistic and I told the Lord today, 'If You are going to heal my son, have someone tell me that I have on a yellow shirt....'"

The man who ended up delivering this prophetic word did not step out of bounds and try to give the woman an interpretation. Surely, the word made little sense to him as he received it—especially as he started going on, describing different things that were yellow. However, because he was obedient and shared only what he sensed the Holy Spirit gave him, the same Holy Spirit brought the prophetic word to life for the woman receiving it by giving her the interpretation. In this situation, God stopped speaking to the man after "yellow." He obediently shared what he was given and the Holy Spirit used the word powerfully in the woman's life.

Questions to Ponder

1. Why do we need to correctly understand the spirit realm?

   _____

   _____

2. What is the difference between the gift of prophecy and the office of a prophet?

   _____

   _____

3. What is the difference between the gifts of the Spirit and the fruits of the Spirit?

_____

_____

4. Who can prophesy?

_____

_____

5. What are the three parts of prophecy?

_____

_____

_____

6. What does the word prophecy mean?

_____

_____

Questions for Group Discussion

1. How can we tell what our giftings, callings, and anointings are?

2. What are the ramifications of getting identity from gifting instead of calling ?

3. What is the difference between a word of prophecy and a word of knowledge?

4. Define what forthtelling and foretelling are.

5. Why is it important for us to only share what we believe the Holy Spirit is telling us—and not give interpretations unless we are first given clear direction by the Lord?

Life Application

Take time now with the Holy Spirit to discover what gifts the Lord has given you. Now ask Him for gifts that you have never walked in. Go to someone who is gifted in the area that you are asking God to gift you in, and have that person lay hands on you and pray for you to receive this gift. Go out and try it!

Let the journey begin!

CHAPTER 3

Learning to Hear the Voice of God

This chapter discusses why the voice of God can sometimes seem elusive or even nonexistent; it investigates the different sources of voices that speak to us from the spirit realm.

God Is Always Speaking

It is natural for you to hear God. When you receive Jesus Christ, you see the Kingdom. You cannot see this Kingdom unless you are first born again. However, once you have received Christ, it is natural for you to start seeing in the Kingdom because you are a believer. This is part of your identity and inheritance. However, the Lord often speaks in mysteries, in riddles, in parables, and in hidden sayings. The Father is talking with us this way all day long; we just need to start tuning in to His frequency.

Jesus died on the Cross not just to forgive our sins but ultimately to bring us into a relationship with God. Communication is probably the single greatest vehicle of any relationship. Although some people have a problem believing that God wants to talk to everybody, most believers understand that true prayer is not just petitioning Heaven with a list of requests, but it is communicating with your Father in Heaven as a true friend.

Jesus said, *"My sheep hear My voice..."* (John 10:27). Prophecy, in its simplest form is merely hearing from the Holy Spirit and repeating what He said. Paul said it this way, *"For you can all prophesy one by one..."* (1 Cor. 14:31). Moses said, *"Would that all the Lord's people were prophets, that the Lord would put His Spirit upon them!"* (Num. 11:29).

Knowledge is power. God doesn't want the prideful to be the powerful; therefore, God hides His word so that only the hungry and the humble have access to His voice. God's word is hidden from the arrogant and the proud.

At that very time He rejoiced greatly in the Holy Spirit, and said, "I praise You, O Father, Lord of heaven and earth, that You have hidden these things from the wise and intelligent and have revealed them to infants. Yes, Father, for this way was well-pleasing in Your sight (Luke 10:21).

The fact is, God is always speaking. The question is, *are we in tune with His voice?*

The Example of the Parables

The parables of Jesus are some of the best examples in Scripture of how the Lord conceals His treasures from the arrogant and proud. Many have been taught that Jesus told parables to demonstrate spiritual principles with natural illustrations. However, Jesus made it clear that He told parables so that people would not understand truth and become powerful. God does not want the prideful to be the powerful. Parables were told not to reveal truth, but to hide it.

And the disciples came and said to Him, "Why do You speak to them in parables?" Jesus answered them, "To you it has been granted to know the mysteries of the kingdom of heaven, but to them it has not been granted. For whoever has, to him more shall be given, and he will have an abundance; but whoever does not have, even what he has shall be taken away from him. Therefore I speak to them in parables; because while seeing they do not see, and while hearing they do not hear, nor do they understand" (Matthew 13:10-13).

But blessed are your eyes, because they see; and your ears, because they hear (Matthew 13:16).

Those who are hungry will search out the treasures that God has hidden for them. The Greek word for "hidden" is *langanw,* which means "to be ignorant or unaware."

When we study the prophets of the Old Testament, we can easily become envious of how clearly they heard God's voice. However, Jesus makes it plain that those who are born again have a tremendous advantage over anyone who lived under the Old Covenant because God's Spirit now resides *within* us and is in constant communication with our spirit.

It is the glory of God to conceal a matter, but the glory of kings is to search out a matter (Proverbs 25:2).

For truly I say to you that many prophets and righteous men desired to see what you see, and did not see it, and to hear what you hear, and did not hear it (Matthew 13:17).

If you have not heard the Lord speaking to you in the past 24 hours, it has little to do with whether or not God still speaks, and everything to do with you understanding your identity. You are a king. You are a queen. Because of this royal identity, you have been given access to *search out a matter*. It is the glory of God to hide things, but it is your glory, as a royal son or a royal daughter of the King, to search out the mysteries. God does not hide things *from* us; He hides them *for* us. God is not being sadistic in hiding things for us; He is evaluating who is really hungry and thirsty for what He has to offer. Remember, Jesus' parables kept knowledge from the wrong people. In the wrong hands, knowledge can puff up; in humble hearts, knowledge stirs even greater hunger and thirst. In fact, as you seek out what God has hidden, the finding process is part of His communication with you. You talk with God and He talks back as you seek out the mysteries and hidden things. He absolutely loves to talk to you. In fact, He wants to talk with you more than you want to listen. The struggle is *not* that God does not speak; it is that we do not understand the language of God. As you start to learn His language, you will find out that He has been speaking all the time—perhaps you just did not recognize it!

God's Goal Is Relationship

God does not want to simply impart information through the gift of prophecy, but rather the goal of all prophetic ministry is to draw us into a deeper relationship with Jesus and His Body. Malachi said that in the last days God would send Elijah the prophet and he will restore the hearts of the fathers to children and the hearts of the children to father's (see Mal. 4:5-6).

Here again we see God's goal for the prophetic ministry deeply rooted in the restoration of relationships. Therefore, if we begin to use the gift of prophecy as a tool to expand our ministry rather than accepting it as an invitation to a deeper relationship with Jesus and His Church, He will "change His language" so that He can tutor us!

As He teaches us His new language, He creates an opportunity for us to draw closer to Himself and closer to His people.

God is always speaking, but His first language is not English.

The Lord Is Always Speaking

The Lord is more determined and excited to speak to us than we are to hear from Him. We must realize that God is always speaking, but He is not human and His first language is not English! If we can grasp this revelation and realize that most of us don't really know how well we see and hear God, we can begin to "tune our receivers to His station."

For example, in the room you are in right now there is music playing all around you. Even if you close your eyes and listen very carefully, you would not hear it. However, by simply turning on a radio, you would perceive what was there all the time. The reason, of course, is that our human bodies were never designed to perceive radio waves.

Likewise, God is always speaking to us! The gift of prophecy is the equipment we need to tap into the spirit realm that exists all around us, even though we can't hear it with our naked ear. The gift of prophecy is like a radio receiver from Heaven. It gives us the ability to hear what God has been speaking to us all along but we were unable to perceive before we received this wonderful gift.

Anointing to Perceive the Supernatural

The king of Israel sent to the place about which the man of God had told him; thus he warned him, so that he guarded himself there, more than once or twice. Now the

heart of the king of Aram was enraged over this thing; and he called his servants and said to them, "Will you tell me which of us is for the king of Israel?" One of his servants said, "No, my lord, O king; but Elisha, the prophet who is in Israel, tells the king of Israel the words that you speak in your bedroom." So he said, "Go and see where he is, that I may send and take him." And it was told him, saying, "Behold, he is in Dothan." He sent horses and chariots and a great army there, and they came by night and surrounded the city. Now when the attendant of the man of God had risen early and gone out, behold, an army with horses and chariots was circling the city. And his servant said to him, "Alas, my master! What shall we do?" So he answered, "Do not fear, for those who are with us are more than those who are with them." Then Elisha prayed and said, "O Lord, I pray, open his eyes that he may see." And the Lord opened the servant's eyes and he saw; and behold, the mountain was full of horses and chariots of fire all around Elisha (2 Kings 6:10-17).

In Second Kings chapter 6, we see that Elisha's calling as a prophet gave him the ability to hear what King Aram would say in secret to his troops. Elisha became a secret weapon to the king of Israel by revealing the plans of this enemy. Then King Aram decides to capture Elisha. On the day of the attack, Elisha's servant comes out of the tent and sees that this enemy army has encircled them. In a panic, his servant runs into the tent and tells Elisha that they are in trouble. Elisha calmly prays for his servant. Immediately, the eyes of his attendant open and he realizes that the mountains are full of horses and chariots of God. The servant's eyes see what was present in the spirit the entire time.

This is the kind of prophetic gift that each of us can receive from God. It causes us to be anointed to perceive what is already happening in the spirit world. Without this prophetic gift, we are like blind people in the Kingdom of God!

The War to Keep Us Deaf

Sometimes we struggle to hear the voice of God because there is a war to keep us spiritually deaf.

In the parable of the sower, Jesus explains why often when God speaks to us, the enemy comes along and tries to convince us that we didn't hear God clearly or that it wasn't God's voice at all! Satan's objective is to prevent us from bringing God's comfort and encouragement to one another through the prophetic word. If he can convince us not to speak the word of the Lord by making us feel foolish, or convince us that it was just our imagination and not a prophetic word, then he has succeeded in stealing the fruit of God's word in someone's life!

The sower sows the word. These are the ones who are beside the road where the word is sown; and when they hear, immediately Satan comes and takes away the word which has been sown in them (Mark 4:14-15).

This principle is also true when it comes to receiving a prophetic word. If the enemy can persuade us that the word spoken to us wasn't really God, then we are robbed of the benefit! The value we place on the word will determine the power we will receive from it.

The value you place on the word determines the power you receive from it.

Valuing the Prophetic Word

The Bible says, *"He who receives a prophet in the name of a prophet shall receive a prophet's reward"* (Matt. 10:41). What is a prophet's reward? The ability to *see* and *hear*. Jesus stood before a crowd and shouted, "HE WHO HAS EYES LET HIM SEE, AND HE WHO HAS EARS LET HIM HEAR!" He was acting as a prophet.

He who receives a prophet in the name of a prophet shall receive a prophet's reward; and he who receives a righteous man in the name of a righteous man shall receive a righteous man's reward (Matthew 10:41).

Everyone who valued Jesus as a prophet and received the words He shouted, received the ability to see and hear. A grace was released with His words that opened their eyes and ears!

Let me give you an example where the value that someone placed on a prophetic word actually determined the power she received from that word:

Gene and Lisa took us to lunch after I spoke at their church one Sunday. They had just adopted two boys after several years of trying to have children. During our meal together, the Lord spoke to me and said, "Tell Lisa that at this time next year she is going to have a baby." I argued with the Lord and told Him I didn't want to give her this word, knowing that she and Gene had received lots of prayer over the years about this issue. He said to me, "If you do not tell her, she will not get pregnant!"

I obediently leaned toward Lisa and quietly told her what the Lord had spoken to me. Although they had been prayed for countless times over the years to conceive children, they received the word of the Lord and Lisa loudly announced, "I'M GOING TO HAVE A BABY!"

A few months later, we came home to a message on our answering machine from Lisa proudly proclaiming, "I'M PREGNANT!"

The next year she had a child, just as the Lord had promised.

Lisa welcomed and positively received the word. As a result, she watched the power of that word produce the intended result in her life—being able to become pregnant.

Valuing the word of the Lord also means that we make time to hear Him. Moses walked past the burning bush in the desert and heard nothing until he stopped and turned aside; we need to set aside time to diligently seek God ourselves with our whole heart.

The angel of the Lord appeared to him in a blazing fire from the midst of a bush; and he looked, and behold, the bush was burning with fire, yet the bush was not consumed. So Moses said, "I must turn aside now and see this marvelous sight, why the bush is not burned up." When the Lord saw that he turned aside to look, God called to him from the midst of the bush and said, "Moses, Moses!" And he said, "Here I am" (Exodus 3:2-4).

But from there you will seek the Lord your God, and you will find Him if you search for Him with all your heart and all your soul (Deuteronomy 4:29).

For the eyes of the Lord move to and fro throughout the earth that He may strongly support those whose heart is completely His. You have acted foolishly in this. Indeed, from now on you will surely have wars (2 Chronicles 16:9).

Even if God speaks audibly from Heaven, some people would only hear it as the sound of thunder. The difference between the deaf and the hearing is not how loudly God speaks, but how open we are to hear Him speak.

"Father, glorify Your name." Then a voice came out of heaven: "I have both glori-fied it, and will glorify it again." So the crowd of people who stood by and heard it were saying that it had thundered; others were saying, "An angel has spoken to Him" (John 12:28-29).

Testing the Spirits

As we are learning to hear the voice of the Holy Spirit, we must realize that not every voice that speaks to us from the spirit realm is from God.

Beloved, do not believe every spirit, but test the spirits to see whether they are from God, because many false prophets have gone out into the world (1 John 4:1).

In First John 4, we are instructed as the "beloved" to *"not believe every spirit, but test the spirits to see whether they are from God, because many false prophets have gone out into the world."* In this passage of Scripture, it is made clear that we—the beloved—are able to hear from spirits other than the Holy Spirit and are warned not to become false prophets by listening to the wrong spirit! Therefore, if it is possible to become a false prophet by listening to the wrong spirit, then it becomes vital to know which voices can speak to us.

Remember, the devil is stealth in how he communicates with *the beloved.* If he were to make himself obvious (the classic horns, pitch fork and red costume approach), no reasonable Christian would give him the time of day. The Bible tells us that, instead, he masquerades as an *"angel of light"* (2 Cor. 11:14) and we are to be aware of his schemes (see 2 Cor. 2:11).

Who Is Speaking to Us?

Voices that speak to us from the spirit realm come from four sources:

1. Our spirit.

2. The Holy Spirit.

3. Evil spirits.

4. Angels.

The Four Sources

- Our spirit: We are a spirit that has a soul and a body. When we are born again, our spirit comes to life making it possible to hear from the spirit realm, but not necessarily hearing from the Holy Spirit. Hearing from our own spirit is still a spiritual experience and being aware of this will help us discern which voice is speaking to us.

- The Holy Spirit: This is God's Spirit, the one with whom we are building a relationship and learning to hear clearly.

- Evil spirits: Spirits from the evil realm can speak to Christians just as they spoke to Jesus when He encountered satan in the wilderness.

- Angels: According to Hebrews chapter 1, these are spirits sent to render service to the saints. Angels also speak to us about the things of God.

Practice Makes Perfect

In the following chapters, there is a more thorough discussion about how to recognize which spirit you are hearing. It takes time to learn to discern what spirit is speaking to you, and there is no substitute for experience.

A banker who had reached the age of retirement was about to be replaced by a young man. Upon his arrival to take the helm from his predecessor, he asked the older man how he became successful. The man replied, "Good decisions."

"How do you make good decisions?" the young man asked.

"Experience," the banker replied.

The young man thought for a moment, and then inquired, "How do you get experience?"

With a warm smile aged with wisdom, he replied, "Bad decisions!"

You cannot grow in the gifts of the Spirit without making mistakes! We gain experience as we step out in faith trying to listen to the Holy Spirit.

Many years ago I went fishing with a man who was several years my senior. We stood on the same bank, using the same bait, and I watched as he caught several fish while I was unsuccessful. Certain that the problem was the pole I was using, I asked if we could swap equipment and he graciously traded poles with me. Still I caught nothing, as he continued to reel in more fish!

I finally decided that the only fish I was going to catch that day was one that was going to commit suicide. He knew what the problem was, but it took me awhile to realize that I did not know how it felt to get a bite.

You see, the older man had experience.

Questions to Ponder

1. List four reasons why we sometimes don't hear God's voice.

_____

_____

_____

_____

2. Why does God sometimes change His language?

_____

_____

3. Why does God hide certain things for His people to seek out?

_____

_____

4. What are the four different voices that try to communicate with us?

_____

_____

_____

_____

5. How does satan affect our ability to hear God?

_____

_____

Questions for Group Discussion

1. What is the relationship between knowing our identity and hearing God's voice? Why is this relationship so important?

2. Why is it important to clearly identify the four different voices we can hear in the spirit realm?

3. Is everything we hear from the spirit realm from the Holy Spirit?

4. Do you think we can prophesy out of the wrong spirit? What would this look like?

Life Application

Having a pure heart is vitally important in communicating with God. The pure in heart see God and can be trusted with His mysteries. Take some time now to ask the Lord to search your heart. Let humility and hunger be your guide.

CHAPTER 4

The Language of God

This chapter is dedicated to understanding the different ways in which God communicates with His people. God's first language is not English. How then does God speak to us? You may be surprised!

The Language of God

God's primary language is not English. It's not Hebrew or Greek either. It is important that we know *how* He speaks in order for us to hear and prophesy accordingly. If we don't recognize the different ways God communicates with His people, we will miss His voice. If we miss God's voice, we will either: a) not move in the gift of prophecy, or, b) we will mistake other voices for God's. Both are places we want to avoid. In this chapter, we will review different ways God communicates with His people. This provides a basic foundation in learning to hear *how* God speaks, and in turn, accurately say what He is saying.

Visions and Dreams

Two of the most common ways the Lord communicates with us is through visions and dreams.

"And it shall be in the last days," God says, "that I will pour forth of My Spirit on all mankind; and your sons and your daughters shall prophesy, and your young men shall see visions, and your old men shall dream dreams; even on my bondslaves, both men and women, I will in those days pour forth of My Spirit and they shall prophesy" (Acts 2:17-18).

Visions

There are two types of visions. The first one is a Vision of the Mind, in which the Lord "projects" images and pictures onto the "screen" of our minds. This can be called a "sanctified imagination" or an imagination that is under the influence of the Holy Spirit. Most often, this is how the Holy Spirit speaks to us. They often appear like hieroglyphics—pictures that require interpretation. So as the Holy Spirit speaks to us through these pictures and images of the mind, we must turn around and ask Him what the pictures mean.

For example, if you were asked to picture a pink elephant, you would see it in your mind's eye. The Holy Spirit uses your mind as a blackboard in which He draws pictures or projects images onto your mind's eye.

The second type of vision is an Open Vision. This is an image that you see with your natural eyes. The following is an example of an open vision.

> Many years ago, I took a group of about 37 kids from our youth group to Santa Cruz, California, for a day on the beach. Among them was our foster daughter, Dee. It happened to be "Muscle Beach Day" and the area was overflowing with people. Our group found a spot to settle and enjoy the day.
>
> Not long after our arrival, I glanced up and saw Dee running along the beach being chased by a man dressed in full leathers. As they ran toward us, I could hear the man shouting to Dee, "I love you! I love you! I'm taking you with me."
>
> She ran to me for protection with this man close behind her. As she knelt next to me in the sand, he reached over and grabbed her by the blouse. He began to shake her, saying loudly, "I love you! I love you!"
>
> Finally, I mustered the courage to grab the man's arm. "That's enough!" I yelled. The man abruptly dropped Dee in the sand, then turned and grabbed me, lifting me up off my knees! He screamed at me, "I love her! I'm taking her with me!"
>
> Just then I saw an open vision appear above his head. Events of his life flashed over him in what appeared to be short video clips! I said to him, "Your mother is in the hospital dying, isn't she?"
>
> "Yes!" he exclaimed.
>
> "Your dad died last year, didn't he?" I shouted.

"Yea," he said.

Then I yelled, "And you blame yourself, don't you?"

With a look of shock and disbelief he said, "Man, you're scaring me!" He turned around and ran away.

I jumped to my feet and chased after him! The whole event turned into quite a scene for the other beachgoers as I caught up with him and tackled him three times. Each time I tackled him, I yelled "YOU NEED JESUS!"

"I know!" he yelled back.

The outrageous event ended when he turned and ran toward his motorcycle gang. He stopped about a hundred yards from me, turned and shouted, "You pray for me!"

"What's your name?"

He shouted back, "Phillip."

Dreams

Dreams are also the language of the Holy Spirit. There are at least two types of dreams. The first is what could be called a Virtual Reality Dream. This occurs while we sleep and remains in our mind after waking.

The following is an example of a virtual reality dream that Nebuchadnezzar had in the days of Daniel. Notice that the dream is symbolic and needs an interpretation.

You, O king, were looking and behold, there was a single great statue; that statue, which was large and of extraordinary splendor, was standing in front of you, and its appearance was awesome. The head of that statue was made of fine gold, its breast and its arms of silver, its belly and its thighs of bronze, its legs of iron, its feet partly of iron and partly of clay. You continued looking until a stone was cut out without hands, and it struck the statue on its feet of iron and clay and crushed them. Then the iron, the clay, the bronze, the silver and the gold were crushed all at the same time and became like chaff from the summer threshing floors; and the wind carried them away so that not a trace of them was found. But the stone that struck the statue became a great mountain and filled the whole earth (Daniel 2:31-35).

The second type of dream can be called a Reality Dream. This is a real experience we have while sleeping that we remember after waking. The spirit world never sleeps. Therefore, our spirit can interact with the spirit world while our soul sleeps. An example of this type of dream is found in Genesis chapter 20, where it states, *"God came to Abimelech in a dream."*

Notice in this reality dream it does not say that he dreamt of God, but rather that he had a real encounter with the Lord and that he remembered it when he woke up.

But God came to Abimelech in a dream of the night, and said to him, "Behold, you are a dead man because of the woman whom you have taken, for she is married" (Genesis 20:3).

Another example of a Reality Dream is in the familiar story of Joseph in Matthew chapter 2. In this event, an angel of the Lord interacts with Joseph while he sleeps.

Now when they had gone, behold, an angel of the Lord appeared to Joseph in a dream and said, "Get up! Take the Child and His mother and flee to Egypt, and remain there until I tell you; for Herod is going to search for the Child to destroy Him" (Matthew 2:13).

Dreams are multifaceted and have many purposes. The Book of Job speaks of dreams that keep us from hell.

Indeed God speaks once, or twice, yet no one notices it. In a dream, a vision of the night, when sound sleep falls on men, while they slumber in their beds, then He opens the ears of men, and seals their instruction, that He may turn man aside from his conduct, and keep man from pride; He keeps back his soul from the pit, and his life from passing over into Sheol (Job 33:14-18).

A friend of ours told us how his son's marriage was restored because of a dream! The night before they were to go to divorce court, his daughter-in-law had a dream. In it she saw the Lord hugging her husband and father-in-law in a field of flowers while she looked on from a distance. In the next scene, she saw herself standing in the field of flowers with Jesus walking toward her. When He reached out to embrace her, she woke up. The next morning, she knew that the Lord wanted her to restore her relationship with her husband. She reconciled their marriage that very day!

Responding to Bad Dreams and Nightmares

If you have a bad dream, there are a few tools you can use to try and determine why.

Origin

Try to identify where the dream came from. Did it come from your spirit? It is possible for your spirit to give you a bad dream. If you worry, you actually create an atmosphere in which your spirit begins to worry. It can continue after you step out of consciousness and into a resting state.

Keep in mind, your spirit is not the Holy Spirit. If you are a worrier, and you are experiencing dreams filled with fear, worry, or anxiety, this does not mean that God is giving you these dreams. Instead, your human spirit is carrying the weight of worry from consciousness into unconsciousness. Your spirit is basically telling you at night what you are thinking about during the day.

Purpose

If you do have a bad dream—like there is a major natural disaster coming—and it is from God, the purpose is not your agreement; it is your intercession. He would give you a dream like that so you could pray against the problem, just like Abraham prayed against the judgment of Sodom and Gomorrah in Genesis 19 and Moses interceded for the Hebrew people in Exodus 32. When God informed both of these men of what was coming, they assumed the position of intercessors. They knew God's character, stood upon His promises, and stood in the gap.

Important Facts to Remember about Dreams

1. Not all dreams are from God. As we learned earlier, we can hear from all four sources of the spirit realm, even in our dreams.

2. Simply because we have powerful and illustrative dreams does not necessarily mean we are prophetic. Remember that wicked people in the Old Testament had dreams. Interpreting dreams is what makes us prophetic.

3. Colors, numbers, and other symbolic occurrences in dreams are very important to the interpretation of the dream. Ultimately the interpretation of dreams belongs to the Lord.

4. A good way for us to increase our supernatural dream life is to lay a notebook or recorder by our bed before going to sleep. Pray to the Lord and tell Him, "Your servant is listening." As soon as you have a dream, write it down or record all of the details that you can remember, including the way you felt about the dream while you were having it.

However, there is a God in heaven who reveals mysteries, and He has made known to King Nebuchadnezzar what will take place in the latter days. This was your dream and the visions in your mind while on your bed (Daniel 2:28).

Communicating with God

God's Still Small Voice

At times, the Lord speaks to us in a still small voice from within our spirit. This is not a booming, audible voice. This can be heard as a passing thought, sudden impression, or internal "sense" of something that God is saying. This still small voice is illustrated in the Book of First Kings. In this account, God is not in the strong wind or the earthquake, but rather He is in the gentle blowing (see 1 Kings 19:11-13).

This is an Old Testament example of the still small voice of God in operation. In the New Testament, we read of the inward witness that the Holy Spirit bears with the human spirit.

The Spirit himself bears witness with our spirit that we are children of God (Romans 8:16 ESV).

Instead of describing an audible voice of God that we hear with our natural ears, we read that the Holy Spirit *"bears witness"* with our human spirits. In this context, the Spirit is confirming that we are the children of God. The same gentle internal assurance that reminds us that we are sons and daughters of God also gently leads us in our everyday lives.

Earlier on in this same chapter, Paul comments that those who are led by the Spirit of God are the sons, or children of God (see Rom. 8:14).

Angels

Angels are other voices from the heavenly realm. Throughout the New Testament angels visited and spoke to people concerning what they should do.

But an angel of the Lord spoke to Philip saying, "Get up and go south to the road that descends from Jerusalem to Gaza" (Acts 8:26).

On the very night when Herod was about to bring him forward, Peter was sleeping between two soldiers, bound with two chains, and guards in front of the door were watching over the prison. And behold, an angel of the Lord suddenly appeared and a light shone in the cell; and he struck Peter's side and woke him up, saying, "Get up quickly." And his chains fell off his hands (Acts 12:6-7).

Trances

Trances are another way God speaks to His people. Trances are much like visions, except when we are in a trance, we are completely unaware of our surroundings. The Greek word for trance means "to be out of your mind." Trances take us out of our natural minds and into God's. Many Christians feel that because people in the occult have trances, all trances are from the devil. The truth is, satan can only copy the things of God. He is not a creator; he is a forger. Counterfeits simply reveal that there is an important source of truth that needs to be properly studied.

On the next day, as they were on their way and approaching the city, Peter went up on the housetop about the sixth hour to pray. But he became hungry and was desiring to eat; but while they were making preparations, he fell into a trance; and he saw the sky opened up, and an object like a great sheet coming down, lowered by four corners to the ground (Acts 10:9-11).

Creation

Creation itself is a voice from the Lord and speaks to us in many ways. The obvious way is that God's creation tells us about who God is. The mountains speak of His strength, the rivers of His provision, and the flowers of His beauty. Another way creation speaks to us is by God actually causing nature to do things that are prophetic acts.

For since the creation of the world His invisible attributes, His eternal power and divine nature, have been clearly seen, being understood through what has been made, so that they are without excuse (Romans 1:20).

The heavens are telling of the glory of God; and their expanse is declaring the work of His hands. Day to day pours forth speech, and night to night reveals knowledge (Psalm 19:1-2).

One year, every time Bethel church would meet to pray, a roadrunner would show up outside the glass door with a lizard in its mouth! This went on for months until we finally realized that the Lord was calling us to go out to the roads, the highways, and the byways and compel the lost to come in! He was literally calling us to evangelism!

One day the roadrunner managed to find his way inside the church. In a desperate attempt to get out of the building, he hit a window and died. I believe the Lord showed us through this event that if we did not reach out to the lost that our church would die.

Scriptures

The Lord can speak to us in our daily reading of the Bible. He can also highlight a verse or story that speaks directly to us about our circumstance. Sometimes, it may even seem as if God is taking a Scripture out of context. It is vital for us to have a basic knowledge of Bible study and context, so we know how everything properly fits in place.

God will never violate His Word, but He will often violate our understanding of His Word. The Holy Spirit may grant us fresh insight or application as we are reading through the Bible. Scripture is a divine blueprint given for instruction, but also for protection. If God gives us fresh insight or new understanding on a verse or portion of Scripture, it is important that it fits within the rest of the body of Scripture. It cannot be in disagreement with the foundation of God's revealed nature and character.`

> *All Scripture is inspired by God and profitable for teaching, for reproof, for correction, for training in righteousness; so that the man of God may be adequate, equipped for every good work* (2 Timothy 3:16-17).

Tongues

Tongues and the interpretation of tongues are both a gift from God and a voice from Heaven. Notice that in First Corinthians 12, it is described as the interpretation of tongues—not the translation of tongues. In other words, the tongue can be quite lengthy while the interpretation of it brief or vice versa. If you like to have things your own way, I suggest you don't pray in tongues! For example, if we were to pray in English, asking the Lord for a Corvette, then start to pray in tongues, the Holy Spirit could be praying, "Lord don't give them a Corvette! They will hurt themselves in that car!"

> *For to one is given the word of wisdom through the Spirit, and to another the word of knowledge according to the same Spirit; to another faith by the same Spirit, and to another gifts of healing by the one Spirit, and to another the effecting of miracles, and to another prophecy, and to another the distinguishing of spirits, to another various kinds of tongues, and to another the interpretation of tongues* (1 Corinthians 12:8-10).

Impressions

Many prophetic people experience discernment through impressions without even realizing it. Oftentimes we can sense an evil spirit on someone just by sitting down next to that person. The evil spirit that is troubling the person who is next to us will begin to trouble us in the same manner. For instance, if a spirit of fear troubles a person in a close geographic area, we can actually begin to feel fearful as well. If we do not realize our prophetic ability and discernment in this area, we can begin to feel very confused or think we are crazy. Within this viewpoint, it can be possible that some of those diagnosed as "bipolar" may actually be experiencing a powerful level of discernment, but do not, unfortunately, know how to navigate this gift properly.

Prophetic Acts

Oftentimes the Lord will direct someone to do a prophetic act, as in the following Scripture example. This was common in the Bible. Jeremiah set a brick in the middle of the city—a prophetic symbol of laying a siege wall against Israel. Agabus tied a belt around himself as a way of showing Paul how he would suffer.

And coming to us, he took Paul's belt and bound his own feet and hands, and said, "This is what the Holy Spirit says: 'In this way the Jews at Jerusalem will bind the man who owns this belt and deliver him into the hands of the Gentiles'" (Acts 21:11).

Signs and Wonders

Many times God will perform signs and wonders as a way to communicate His love or direction.

So Gideon said to Him, "If now I have found favor in Your sight, then show me a sign that it is You who speak with me. Please do not depart from here, until I come back to You, and bring out my offering and lay it before You." And He said, "I will remain until you return." Then Gideon went in and prepared a young goat and unleavened bread from an ephah of flour; he put the meat in a basket and the broth in a pot, and brought them out to him under the oak and presented them. The angel of God said to him, "Take the meat and the unleavened bread and lay them on this rock, and pour out the broth." And he did so. Then the angel of the Lord put out the end of the staff that was in his hand and touched the meat and the unleavened bread; and fire sprang up from the rock and consumed the meat and the unleavened bread. Then the angel of the Lord vanished from his sight (Judges 6:17-21).

Distinguishing (Discerning) of Spirits

...and to another the distinguishing of spirits... (1 Corinthians 12:10).

This is one of the nine gifts of the Spirit—also referred to as the discerning of spirits (depending on the Bible version). If someone is troubled by an evil spirit and we have the gift of discernment, when we get close to that person, we will start picking up traces of the spirit that is at work in his or her life. This works for either angelic or demonic spirits. Through the Holy Spirit, God will give you special insight into what forces are at work in an individual's life so you can appropriately minister to that person.

Mind Reading

Many immediately assume that "mind reading" is solely attached to occult, New Age, or ESP phenomena. These are counterfeit expressions of something authentic. In the Gospels, we see Jesus reading people's thoughts and using that information to interact with them. Jesus demonstrated this prophetic ability over and over again in His ministry. He would answer questions that no one asked because He knew what was on their minds.

> *But He knew their thoughts and said to them, "Any kingdom divided against itself is laid waste; and a house divided against itself falls"* (Luke 11:17).

There are times when someone is ministering to a person prophetically and can read that person's thoughts. Not realizing what just took place, the person ministering may begin to prophesy to the person receiving ministry *their* desires instead of the heart of the Lord. Understanding that prophetic people can sometimes read the minds of others helps to keep this dynamic out of our prophecies.

Also, there is no special "mind reading" gift. We should not go out and try to read people's thoughts. This is special insight that the Holy Spirit gives to us as He wills.

Circumstances

God can speak to us and direct us through the circumstances of our lives. This dynamic occurs as God opens and closes the doors of opportunity. It is easy to misunderstand this principle and think that any time we come up against an obstacle in our lives that God cannot be in it. However, keep in mind that any time we are doing something for God, the devil will oppose us!

I know your deeds. Behold, I have put before you an open door which no one can shut, because you have a little power, and have kept My word, and have not denied My name (Revelation 3:8).

Dance

Many churches have dancers as part of their worship team. Oftentimes, God will begin to choreograph a supernatural, spontaneous dance, which is actually a prophetic act that the Lord is speaking to us through the dance.

Then the virgin will rejoice in the dance, and the young men and the old, together, for I will turn their mourning into joy and will comfort them and give them joy for their sorrow (Jeremiah 31:13).

Prophetic Songs

Often during worship the Lord will give someone a spontaneous song that is from God to the people. It is common for God to give the prophetic singer the lyrics and the melody.

Let the word of Christ richly dwell within you, with all wisdom teaching and admonishing one another with psalms and hymns and spiritual songs, singing with thankfulness in your hearts to God (Colossians 3:16).

Prophetic Body Checks

Sometimes the Lord will communicate His desire to heal someone else's body by causing pain or a sensation in a certain part of the prophetic person's body; it typically correlates to the sickness in the person God wants to heal. If we receive this kind of information from the Holy Spirit, it is important that we are aware of what pain or discomfort is common to us. Without clarification, we could mistakenly confuse our pain with a word of knowledge for healing.

Spiritual Happenings

Spiritual happenings are another way God speaks to us. These are supernatural incidents that correlate with natural events. Notice that in the Book of Numbers, Aaron's rod came alive after being dead, and bore blossoms and ripe almonds as a sign from God that he was anointed to be a leader of Israel.

Speak to the sons of Israel, and get from them a rod for each father's household: twelve rods, from all their leaders according to their fathers' households. You shall write each name on his rod, and write Aaron's name on the rod of Levi; for there is one rod for the head of each of their fathers' households. You shall then deposit them in the tent of meeting in front of the testimony, where I meet with you. It will come about that the rod of the man whom I choose will sprout. Thus I will lessen from upon Myself the grumblings of the sons of Israel, who are grumbling against you. Moses therefore spoke to the sons of Israel, and all their leaders gave him a rod apiece, for each leader according to their fathers' households, twelve rods, with the rod of Aaron among their rods. So Moses deposited the rods before the Lord in the tent of the testimony. Now on the next day Moses went into the tent of the testimony; and behold, the rod of Aaron for the house of Levi had sprouted and put forth buds and produced blossoms, and it bore ripe almonds (Numbers 17:2-8).

Some time ago, every time I entered a worship service, I noticed that my watch gained an hour. After purchasing three different watches, all of which gained an hour only during worship, I finally asked the Lord what this could mean.

He said, "It's later than you think."

Questions to Ponder

1. What is one way to increase your dream life?

   _____

   _____

   _____

2. How is the discerning of spirits a gift from God?

   _____

   _____

3. What is one of the most common mistakes people make when they allow God to direct them through circumstances?

_____

_____

4. Name two ways that creation can speak to us.

_____

_____

5. What is the difference between a vision and a trance?

_____

_____

Questions for Group Discussion

1. What is the most common way that God speaks to you personally? (Based on the different categories you studied.)

2. What is the difference between dreams and visions?

3. Why is it important for us to not interpret a dream or vision unless God gives us the interpretation?

4. Was there a way God communicates to His people that was surprising to you?

5. Is there anything that has occurred in your life that, after reading this chapter, you now recognize as God speaking to you?

Life Application

Go on a Holy Spirit adventure! You can do this by simply taking a few minutes to pray and ask the Holy Spirit to show you where to go and who to talk to. He is eager to accompany you on this exploit. You will learn how to hear His voice—be ready for some surprises along the way!

CHAPTER 5

Judging and Receiving Prophetic Words

Developing a safe environment for the gifts of the Spirit to operate effectively is important. This chapter examines the reasons why prophecy needs to be judged and the proper criteria by which prophetic ministry should be evaluated. We will also explore the correct way to receive prophetic words.

Prophetic Balance: Holy Spirit and Human Personality

Often we think that in order to share a prophetic word, it must be "wholly God." This perspective eliminates the need for faith, and also assumes that in order for us to prophesy, we need the entire word, from start to finish. This is rare.

Prophecy typically begins with an unction. A picture. An image. It starts with something, in part, but often does not contain the full message. This is an invitation for us to step out, say what we believe the Holy Spirit is saying, and trust Him to guide and direct us as we open our mouths and share the message.

When God stops speaking, you need to step out in faith. His voice will often give you the launching pad for sharing a prophetic word. But time after time, as I have operated in prophetic ministry, the Holy Spirit will give me something to start with and it is my responsibility, as a mouthpiece, to speak out what I have received. More often comes as we share the little or part we received. However, if we are waiting for the entire message to come to us before we step out and prophesy, we will rarely, if ever, operate in the prophetic ministry.

Of course we want to faithfully share what God is saying. We do not want to add our human reasoning, interpretations, and advice to the words of the Holy Spirit. This is not license to hear God's voice, receive His word—in part—and then go on to *add* our ideas to what God is saying.

What may happen is that you receive a concept from God, or get a word, or a Scripture comes to mind, or you see an image, or imagine a symbol—this is your starting point. The starting point for prophetic ministry is understanding the different ways God speaks to us, as we studied in the previous chapter. It is important, however, that you understand where the message is coming to: *you.* The Holy Spirit is speaking to you, which means His message will be filtered through your experience, the teaching you have received in your life, your ethnic culture, national origin, gender, etc. All of these things are part of who you are, and not all of them are negative. Could it be that the filtering process is part of the prophetic experience? In other words, the Holy Spirit knows who you are. He is aware of your background, your heritage, and your gender. He knows that His message will be filtered through some of these layers. This is not a bad thing! Remember, the message is being "filtered," not altered or adjusted.

Understanding the way God speaks to us is important.

Consider the Old Testament prophets. God speaks to Jeremiah—the weeping prophet. He cries all the time. On the other hand, we do not observe someone like Elijah crying for anyone. God actually uses the personalities of the people He speaks through to communicate His message. When some of us prophesy, there might be repeated themes in the different messages and words we share. If we are prophesying out of the right spirit, we are not adding anything to what the Holy Spirit is saying. When someone has a certain "prophetic style" or a specific theme can be traced throughout their different words, this reveals how God actually takes people He created, and puts *our unique flavor* in His message. He entrusts His words to different people because He knows *how* they will go about sharing His message.

For a prophetic word to be *wholly God*, it does not mean that the word has to be a 100 percent translation. Remember, the process often begins with a single word or image. We step out, using what He has shown us, and confidently trust the rest of the process to the

Holy Spirit. Remember, He is using a human being as His mouthpiece. He is well aware of what He is getting into!

Judge All Prophecy

In First Thessalonians, Paul instructs us not to despise prophetic utterances. Any of us who have had experience with prophetic ministry can easily understand why Paul would bring up the subject of despising prophetic ministry. Many churches, in response to poor prophetic ministry, have altogether eliminated the gifts of the Spirit from their services and teachings. We also learn that a prophetic word should be examined carefully, and that we should hold on to what is found to be good.

Do not quench the Spirit; do not despise prophetic utterances. But examine everything carefully; hold fast to that which is good (1 Thessalonians 5:19-21).

Paul's exhortation, however, is that the Kingdom of God does not consist of words but of power (see 1 Cor. 4:20). He also reminds us, *"that your faith should not rest on the wisdom of men, but on the power of God"* (1 Cor. 2:5).

We must embrace the prophetic while also being careful to evaluate or judge all prophetic ministry—this includes the messages of those prophesying and also those occupying the position of a prophet. No one is exempt.

Let two or three prophets speak, and let the others pass judgment (1 Corinthians 14:29).

No matter what level you are on in the prophetic ministry—from someone sharing a prophetic word to a nationally known and respected prophet—you are not exempt from your words being judged.

Prophets Can Make Mistakes Without Being False Prophets

Many people in the church have a problem believing that a real prophet of God can make a mistake while prophesying. They assume only false prophets make mistakes. In First

Corinthians, we are exhorted to let two or three prophets speak in a service and to let the other prophets offer judgment on the word.

The truth is that even the apostles and prophets in the Bible gave prophecies that were not entirely accurate.

One example is in Acts 21 with Agabus the prophet. He is arguably one of, if not the, most famous prophets in the New Testament. Even though he was able to accurately predict a famine, he also prophesied that the Jews in Jerusalem would bind Paul and hand him over to the Gentiles.

As we were staying there for some days, a prophet named Agabus came down from Judea. And coming to us, he took Paul's belt and bound his own feet and hands, and said, "This is what the Holy Spirit says: 'In this way the Jews at Jerusalem will bind the man who owns this belt and deliver him into the hands of the Gentiles'" (Acts 21:10-11).

What actually happened: the Gentiles rescued Paul from the Jews.

At once he took along some soldiers and centurions and ran down to them; and when they saw the commander and the soldiers, they stopped beating Paul. Then the commander came up and took hold of him, and ordered him to be bound with chains; and he began asking who he was and what he had done (Acts 21:32-33).

In verse 30 of Acts chapter 22, the commander turned Paul over to the Jews. This was the opposite of what Agabus prophesied.

But on the next day, wishing to know for certain why he had been accused by the Jews, he released him and ordered the chief priests and all the Council to assemble, and brought Paul down and set him before them (Acts 22:30).

It is obvious that Agabus was correct about the heart of what God was saying, but he got the details slightly mixed up.

Another example of a prophetic word that was not entirely accurate can be found in Acts 27:10. Here Paul says, in essence, "If we sail on, we will lose the ship and we will all die."

However, later in verses 22 and 23 of Acts chapter 27, Paul is corrected by an angel who says, *"There will be no loss of life among you, but only of the ship."* This may seem like a minor mistake unless you happen to be one of the men on the ship!

Theologically, some people quote Deuteronomy chapter 18 as evidence that a prophet is false if some of their prophecies are inaccurate. We need to understand the difference between the Old Testament and New Testament prophetic ministry in order to make sense of what verses like this are saying.

I will raise up a prophet from among their countrymen like you, and I will put My words in his mouth, and he shall speak to them all that I command him (Deuteronomy 18:18).

But the prophet who speaks a word presumptuously in My name which I have not commanded him to speak, or which he speaks in the name of other gods, that prophet shall die (Deuteronomy 18:20).

Old Testament versus New Testament Prophecy

In the Old Testament, prophets *received* the word of the Lord.

In the New Testament, prophetic people *perceive* the word of the Lord.

In the Old Testament, the Spirit of God did not live inside humans, nor had the human spirit been brought to life. This happens during the new-birth process when we receive Christ. Therefore when prophets in the Old Testament heard from God, it was an occasion because Christ was not living inside them.

In this new dispensation, our spirit is alive and the Holy Spirit lives inside us. Now, as Christians, we daily interact with the spirit world. It is easy to confuse the Holy Spirit's words with our newly regenerated spirit's words. Remember, now we can have a spiritual experience without the Holy Spirit's participation, for we are a spirit trying to have a temporary, human experience.

The reason why prophecy in the Old Testament was severely judged (except to kill the prophet or to wait to see if the prophecy would come to pass) is because the people were spiritually dead. They had no spiritual paradigm by which to process spiritual information. In those days, their judgment was based on whether or not they liked the word. It is easy to see why, in the Old Testament, they killed prophets who misled them. These men had tremendous influence over their people, as well as entire countries.

In the New Testament Church, however, the Christian who receives the word has as much responsibility to judge the word as the one who gave it because both the giver and receiver have the same Holy Spirit living inside them.

Developing a Refuse Gate

Some people are overly sensitive to negative spiritual experiences. They spend their lives trying to stay safe and clean. God has made His people durable. In the city of Jerusalem there was a refuse gate—the area where all of the city garbage was dumped. Our own human body has a system of elimination that disposes of anything that does not nourish it. There is a need in the Body of Christ for a system of elimination as well. Otherwise, we will be poisoned by poor ministry or worse yet, starved to death by those who refuse the Holy Spirit's work because they are afraid that someone might "slime" them.

Sadly, one of the barriers to preventing a healthy prophetic culture is the fear of receiving a "bad prophetic word." We need to mature to the point where we learn how to disregard a word that does not sit with our spirit, or align with God's Word. Also, we should approach these individuals and let them know that what they said was not good. If it hurt us, we need to let them know—yes, for our benefit, but also for their growth and development. People will continue to deliver bad, incorrect, or off prophetic words to the degree that we do not engage them constructively and in love.

Even though we will always remain "works in progress" this side of Heaven, we can take certain steps to developing a healthy environment where the prophetic can flow freely and we can openly interact with each other about both our "hits and misses." Often, people mean well, they just don't know what they are doing and need to be told. It is important for us to recognize that this approach of correction and discussion is mainly for those with whom we have a relationship.

Order in the Church

The Bible tells us that the gifts of the Spirit should be practiced properly and in order. The first part of this commandment is that they should be practiced! There is no need for order if you never allow the Spirit to move. If you have ever witnessed the birth of a child, you will realize that God's idea of "decently and in order" is far different from ours. New life can be messy!

> *But all things must be done properly and in an orderly manner* (1 Corinthians 14:40).

Wherever people are ministering to one another there will be messes. Messes are one of the signs that life is happening. The most orderly place on the planet is the graveyard; but there is no life there.

> *Where no oxen are, the manger is clean, but much revenue comes by the strength of the ox* (Proverbs 14:4).

Think of what the manger is full of when there is much increase!

This does not mean that allowing the manifestation of the gifts of the Spirit in the church should be without guidelines. Jesus said that He pours new wine into new wineskins. He did not say that He pours new wine into no wineskins. In First Corinthians chapter 14, Paul instructs us to have order in the church. He tells us, *"the spirits of prophets are subject to prophets"* (1 Cor. 14:32). This means that no one can say that the Holy Spirit made him or her act in a disruptive manner. The Holy Spirit subjects Himself to us.

It is the responsibility of the church leadership to establish guidelines and boundaries. When this is done, the Spirit will move inside of these when He is invited to. This becomes the new wineskin, which of course must be flexible.

Guidelines for Judging Prophetic Words

1. The word must be congruent with the Scriptures as well as the heart of Father God. There are three categories of prophetic revelation: biblical, extra-biblical, and anti-biblical.

Biblical

All of the Bible is in God, but not all of God is in the Bible. Scripture is our blueprint to evaluate whether or not a word contains the DNA of God. Even though the entirety of who God is and how He operates is not contained in Scripture, I believe the Holy Spirit gave humankind the Bible to protect our understanding from deception. His character is in there. His nature is revealed.

Extra-Biblical

You may say, "I don't believe in things that are extra-biblical" (meaning a practice or process that is not specifically defined in the Bible). Yes you do! Perhaps three quarters of what you practice in your everyday Christian life is not specifically outlined in the Bible. For example, what we know as the "altar call," where we invite people to raise their hands, pray a prayer, and come to the front of a church is not specifically presented in Scripture. However, the principles that govern why we have altar calls are clearly there. Think about it. As far as we can see, no one was instructed to "pray a prayer" after an evangelist or pastor in the New Testament in order to receive salvation. This is an extra-biblical practice that leads to a very biblical result: salvation. In Jesus' day, no one talked about praying a prayer or coming forward in a church. Jesus never said, "If you want to be My disciple, pray this prayer." No. He simply said, "Follow Me."

An example of an extra-biblical prophetic word would be something like the Holy Spirit saying, "Go to Africa," or "Work at this job" or "Move to this city" or "Write these words to this person." While none of these instructions are specifically written in the Bible, the Author of Scripture, the Holy Spirit, is the One who gives us clearance on whether or not the word is of God or not. We cannot go to the Bible and judge whether or not we are supposed to go to Africa. Even if someone gives you a prophetic word that comes directly out of Scripture, oftentimes the application is extra-biblical. For example, someone may say, "I see Isaiah 60 over you." This Scripture was written to a specific group of people, in a unique time period and placed in a strategic context. When it is applied to you and your life, it becomes extra-biblical.

Anti-Biblical

Anti-biblical simply means against the Bible. Read how the apostle Paul considers this type of "revelation":

But even if we, or an angel from heaven, should preach to you a gospel contrary to what we have preached to you, he is to be accursed! (Galatians 1:8)

It does not matter what type of spiritual experience you had or who appeared to you in an open vision. If the message you received is against what is clearly presented in Scripture, it is anti-biblical and must be rejected.

2. It must bear witness with the spirit of the one who receives it.

The Spirit Himself testifies with our spirit that we are children of God (Romans 8:16).

3. The fruit of the prophetic word must be that the person receiving it is brought closer to God and His people.

More than that, I count all things to be loss in view of the surpassing value of knowing Christ Jesus my Lord, for whom I have suffered the loss of all things, and count them but rubbish so that I may gain Christ, and may be found in Him, not having a righteousness of my own derived from the Law, but that which is through faith in Christ, the righteousness which comes from God on the basis of faith, that I may know Him and the power of His resurrection and the fellowship of His sufferings, being conformed to His death (Philippians 3:8-10).

4. The prophets and leadership should be in agreement with the word and its interpretation and application.

Obey your leaders and submit to them, for they keep watch over your souls as those who will give an account. Let them do this with joy and not with grief, for this would be unprofitable for you (Hebrews 13:17).

5. The interpretation of any prophetic revelation belongs to God, not to humankind. Therefore, we also need the Holy Spirit's anointing to know the meaning of the word as well as what to do with it.

But know this first of all, that no prophecy of Scripture is a matter of one's own interpretation, for no prophecy was ever made by an act of human will, but men moved by the Holy Spirit spoke from God (2 Peter 1:20-21).

Sometimes when we receive a prophetic word, we don't realize what it means until after it has been fulfilled. An example of this is found in Exodus chapter 3 where Moses asks God for a sign so he can know for sure that it is God who is sending him. The Lord spoke to him and said, "After you bring the people out of Egypt, you will worship at this mountain."

But Moses said to God, "Who am I, that I should go to Pharaoh, and that I should bring the sons of Israel out of Egypt?" And He said, "Certainly I will be with you, and this shall be the sign to you that it is I who have sent you: when you have brought the people out of Egypt, you shall worship God at this mountain" (Exodus 3:11-12).

Jesus' prophecy about His own death and resurrection was not understood until after He rose from the dead.

Jesus answered them, "Destroy this temple, and in three days I will raise it up." The Jews then said, "It took forty-six years to build this temple, and will You raise it up in three days?" But He was speaking of the temple of His body. So when He was raised from the dead, His disciples remembered that He said this; and they believed the Scripture and the word which Jesus had spoken (John 2:19-22).

Judging the Interpretation

It is easy to misjudge a prophetic word by believing that it relates to our immediate circumstances or something close to our heart that we are hoping for. This can be called selective hearing!

I have given thousands of prophetic words to people over the years, and I am sometimes amazed at what people think they hear me say. Occasionally, what people hear from prophecy and what the actual word is are not even close to being the same thing!

A vivid example of this sort of misinterpretation is in the account of Matthew chapter 16. The disciples had neglected to bring bread. When Jesus says to them, *"Watch out and beware of the leaven of the Pharisees and Sadducees,"* they thought He was scolding them for forgetting the bread. How did they get that from the word, *"Beware of the leaven of the Pharisees and Sadducees?"* They read their circumstances into His word!

And Jesus said to them, "Watch out and beware of the leaven of the Pharisees and Sadducees." They began to discuss this among themselves, saying, "He said that because we did not bring any bread." But Jesus, aware of this, said, "You men of little faith, why do you discuss among yourselves that you have no bread? Do you not yet understand or remember the five loaves of the five thousand, and how many baskets full you picked up? Or the seven loaves of the four thousand, and how many large baskets full you picked up? How is it that you do not understand that I did not speak to you concerning bread? But beware of the leaven of the Pharisees and Sadducees." Then they understood that He did not say to beware of the leaven of bread, but of the teaching of the Pharisees and Sadducees (Matthew 16:6-12).

Looking Into the Heart of the Matter

In the Book of Exodus, God tells Moses that He is going to kill the people Moses led out of Egypt because they are obstinate and evil. Moses argues with the Lord that they are the Lord's people who were led out of Egypt. After a debate, God changes His mind and leads the people into the Promised Land. Why would God prophesy to Moses something He didn't really want to do? Sometimes when God speaks to us, He is testing our hearts more than He is revealing our destiny. God was determining if Moses had the heart it would take to lead His people.

So the Lord changed His mind about the harm which He said He would do to His people (Exodus 32:14).

Sometimes when God speaks He is testing our hearts
rather than revealing our destinies.

Traditionally, the Church has had a one-dimensional way to judge prophecy. But God is calling us into a deeper relationship with Him. This will lead us into new ways of judging prophetic ministry.

The Lord said to Moses, "I have seen this people, and behold, they are an obstinate people. Now then let Me alone, that My anger may burn against them and that I may destroy them; and I will make of you a great nation." Then Moses entreated the Lord his God, and said, "O Lord, why does Your anger burn against Your people whom You have brought out from the land of Egypt with great power and with a mighty hand? Why should the Egyptians speak, saying, 'With evil intent He brought them out to kill them in the mountains and to destroy them from the face of the earth'? Turn from Your burning anger and change Your mind about doing harm to Your people. Remember Abraham, Isaac, and Israel, Your servants to whom You swore by Yourself, and said to them, 'I will multiply your descendants as the stars of the heavens, and all this land of which I have spoken I will give to your descendants, and they shall inherit it forever.'" So the Lord changed His mind about the harm which He said He would do to His people (Exodus 32:9-14).

Here is another example of prophetic ministry that was received in an unusual manner. Referring again to Agabus the prophet, he ministers to the apostle Paul by telling him that if he goes to Jerusalem he will be bound and arrested. Paul doesn't think the prophetic word means that God doesn't want him to go, but rather that God is telling him to count the cost. This emphasizes the need to look into the heart of God to truly understand what He wants instead of what He seems to be saying.

As we were staying there for some days, a prophet named Agabus came down from Judea. And coming to us, he took Paul's belt and bound his own feet and hands, and said, "This is what the Holy Spirit says: 'In this way the Jews at Jerusalem will bind the man who owns this belt and deliver him into the hands of the Gentiles.'" When we had heard this, we as well as the local residents began begging him not to go up to Jerusalem. Then Paul answered, "What are you doing, weeping and

breaking my heart? For I am ready not only to be bound, but even to die at Jerusalem for the name of the Lord Jesus" (Acts 21:10-13).

How to Receive Prophetic Words

When we are given a prophetic word, we must judge the word to make sure it is from God. The next step is for us to learn how to receive the word. It is important to know when to get out of the way and when to prepare the way. This point is illustrated in the life of Abraham and Sarah in Genesis chapters 16-21. God told them that they were going to have a son. But the years rolled on and still they had no children.

It is worth pausing here and noting that God is on a different timetable than we are. In fact, He is completely outside of time, while we have been placed within its confines and limitations. We have a beginning and an end; God does not. God lives in eternity and He is able to see the end from the beginning. When He gives us a word, we cannot assume that its fulfillment will take place within twenty-four hours. Jesus said that He was coming quickly. Two thousand years have passed and we are still waiting. Perceived delay does not mean denial. Again, we need to recognize that when we received a prophetic word we are actually receiving a word from a Source that is outside of time and in eternity. God may give you a word today that will be fulfilled twenty years later. It is actually in God's nature to talk to us about our futures, but not have anything happen…yet. This was definitely the case with Abraham and Sarah.

Unfortunately, they decided to help God bring about His promise by having Abraham sleep with Hagar, Sarah's maid. This resulted in Hagar giving birth to Ishmael. Ishmael persecuted the child of promise the rest of his days (see Gal. 4:29).

Finally God came to Abraham and Sarah and prophesied to them that they were going to have a son the following year. Sarah laughed and said, *"After I have become old, shall I have pleasure, my lord being old also?"* (Gen. 18:12). But despite her doubt, Isaac was born the following year. The amazing thing to remember here is that Isaac was not born through immaculate conception. Abraham and Sarah had to participate in the union of marriage in order to have Isaac. In one respect, they created an Ishmael by trying to make the prophetic word come to pass, yet they still had to co-labor with God to see His promise become a reality.

God seldom does things all by Himself.

We need to realize that God seldom does things all by Himself. He often requires us to be involved with Him to see our destinies fulfilled. The key here is to allow the Holy Spirit to show us what part He wants us to play and what part God has reserved for Himself. Otherwise, we will create Ishmaels who will persecute our Isaacs!

We also must learn how to receive prophetic ministry multi-dimensionally. In other words, when God speaks to us about doing something new, He doesn't necessarily want us to stop our current activity. Usually, He wants to add to our responsibilities. This is illustrated in the parable of the talents. When the stewards were faithful with few talents, they received more for they had carefully tended what they had been given. We need to be careful how we apply prophetic words to our lives because God wants to bless us abundantly.

To one he gave five talents, to another, two, and to another, one, each according to his own ability; and he went on his journey. Immediately the one who had received the five talents went and traded with them, and gained five more talents. In the same manner the one who had received the two talents gained two more. But he who received the one talent went away, and dug a hole in the ground and hid his master's money.

Now after a long time the master of those slaves came and settled accounts with them. The one who had received the five talents came up and brought five more talents, saying, "Master, you entrusted five talents to me. See, I have gained five more talents." His master said to him, "Well done, good and faithful slave. You were faithful with a few things, I will put you in charge of many things; enter into the joy of your master."

Also the one who had received the two talents came up and said, "Master, you entrusted two talents to me. See, I have gained two more talents." His master said to him, "Well done, good and faithful slave. You were faithful with a few things, I will put you in charge of many things; enter into the joy of your master" (Matthew 25:15-23).

An Invitation to Friendship

In looking at both Abraham and Moses, we see two men who have significant influence with God. Consider that both men lived before the New Covenant. They did not have access to what you and I enjoy every day—the indwelling Holy Spirit—and yet, their prayers changed outcomes significantly. The Bible calls both men *friends* of God. With friendship, comes interaction, intimacy, and influence. These men interacted with God at a dimension above the rest (in the Old Testament), which brought them into close intimacy with Him. This intimate knowledge of God's character and His ways gave Moses and Abraham boldness to interact with Him the way that they did.

Remember, a prophetic word is *not* always God determining our destiny for us. With Moses and Abraham, they received prophetic words and received them as opportunities to intercede for different outcomes. God told Abraham that He was going to wipe Sodom and Gomorrah off the face of the earth. Abraham's response was to approach God, boldly, and remind Him of His mercy. Think of the freedom that Abraham must have felt in order to approach God like he did. Even though he did not talk God out of destroying the cities, he felt the freedom to try.

In Exodus, God told Moses that He was going to wipe out all of the Hebrew people (who He just delivered out of Egypt) and start over with him. Moses interceded and the people were spared.

Just because we hear from God, this does not mean that the word we hear is destiny defining; it could actually be our invitation to change the future. What separates Abraham and Moses from many people in the church today is that these men in the Old Testament did not see God as an unapproachable cosmic ruler who did not ask for input. Does God *need* our input? Not at all. However, there are times where He actually calls us to participate in the process.

> **Prophecy is about friendship with God.**

This is why prophecy is so important. When all is said and done, it is about friendship with God. It is about knowing Him and tuning our ears to hear His voice. We know His voice because it reflects His character, and we get to know His character in the place of friendship.

Prophecy is also a process where God speaks to us, and we have the opportunity to talk back. Not in rebellion. Not in disobedience. Not in the way we commonly think of "talking back." God shares His thoughts and desires with His friends. As friends, we get to respond and say, "How about this, God? Can I have some say in this process and decision?" If the Lord says, "No," it is clearly no. The problem is that we have long assumed that it is always "no." God may want to expose us to new levels of relationship with Him through a process of communicating back and forth—talking, listening, and then talking back and listening again.

Prophetic words like these are invitations to a relationship. However, like all other prophetic words, they are subject to careful review and evaluation as well.

Questions to Ponder

1. What is the difference between judging Old Testament and New Testament prophecy?

_____

_____

2. How is it possible to have a prophetic word from God that may have parts of it that are inaccurate?

_____

_____

3. Is it possible for a word to be scriptural but not from God? (Refer to Luke 4.)

_____

_____

4. Name the five ways that prophecy is to be judged.

_____

_____

_____

_____

_____

5. Give two examples of people who heard from God and ended up asking Him to change His mind about a situation. What does this show you about the prophetic?

_____

_____

Discussion Questions

1. How does the Holy Spirit use human vessels (filtered through our personalities) to communicate a prophetic word?

2. What are some of the ways we should work with people who continually give inaccurate words?

3. What should we do if we give a prophetic word to someone in our leadership and they believe the word is wrong even though we believe we heard from God?

4. What is the difference between biblical, extra-biblical, and anti-biblical revelation?

5. What should we do if we receive a prophetic word that does not immediately come to pass in our lives?

6. Is a prophetic word always a word where God is sovereignly defining our destiny? Do we have any say in the process?

Life Application

Team up with a couple of other prophetic people. Prophesy and give words of knowledge to each other. Ask those who received the words to judge them for accuracy. This is not the time to extend mercy to each other! Honesty is very important as we learn to hear the Holy Spirit's voice. We learn just as much from being wrong as we do from being right. So if the word that we received was not accurate, it is right and proper to tell the person who prophesied. We should also include the reason why we do not believe the word, or portions of it, are from God.

CHAPTER 6

Receiving and Ministering in the Gift of Prophecy

The previous chapters explored the Gift of Prophecy and how to allow the Holy Spirit to flow through your life. This chapter reveals how to receive and grow in the Holy Spirit's gifts.

How to Receive

The most common way to receive spiritual gifts is by having someone who is already gifted lay hands on you and pray for an impartation of the gift or gifts of the Holy Spirit.

> *For I long to see you so that I may impart some spiritual gift to you, that you may be established* (Romans 1:11).

> *And when Paul had laid his hands upon them, the Holy Spirit came on them, and they began speaking with tongues and prophesying* (Acts 19:6).

> *Do not neglect the spiritual gift within you, which was bestowed on you through prophetic utterance with the laying on of hands by the presbytery* (1 Timothy 4:14).

One of the elementary teachings of Christ is impartation of spiritual gifts through the laying on of hands. This principle is found in the very roots of Jewish culture. In fact, it was the reason why Jacob was blessed and Esau was cursed. The significance of the laying on of hands is further demonstrated in the Book of Hebrews in that it is mentioned in the same context as resurrection and eternal judgment.

BASIC TRAINING FOR THE PROPHETIC MINISTRY

Therefore leaving the elementary teaching about the Christ, let us press on to maturity, not laying again a foundation of repentance from dead works and of faith toward God, of instruction about washings and laying on of hands, and the resurrection of the dead and eternal judgment (Hebrews 6:1-2).

Equipped for Battle

This charge I entrust to you, Timothy, my child, in accordance with the prophecies previously made about you, that by them you may wage the good warfare (1 Timothy 1:18 ESV).

One of the reasons it is so important for us to receive prophetic words is because they sustain and equip us through battle. Prophetic ministry actually gives you weapons to defend yourself against the evil schemes of the enemy. Paul knew this as he was writing his letter to young Timothy. His goal was to help Timothy keep perspective during the difficult times. In fact, Paul writes to him twice and talks to him about taking prophetic words that were given to him and using these to fight against the strategies of the enemy. These strategies are age-old: lying and deception.

Paul was encouraging Timothy to revisit the former prophetic words that he had received and use them as weapons during times of assault. If we remember who we are, and whose we are, we have what it takes to win nearly every battle. Trials intensify in our lives and position us for discouragement when we forget who we are, and who we belong to. If the enemy can blind us from Truth, he has got us right where he wants us. Prophetic words remind us of our destiny. They confirm our calling. They encourage, edify, and console. They tell us how big God is, how strong we are in Christ, and how small and defeated the devil truly is.

The Role of Grace

Through grace we receive the abilities of the Holy Spirit. These abilities equip us to work in the harvest. Grace is not just undeserved favor; it is also the operational power of God.

But to each one of us grace was given according to the measure of Christ's gift. ...And He gave some as apostles, and some as prophets, and some as evangelists,

and some as pastors and teachers, for the equipping of the saints for the work of service, to the building up of the body of Christ (Ephesians 4:7,11-12).

Determining the Strength of Your Gift

Although the gifts are imparted through the laying on of hands, you still must receive them from the one who imparts them to you by faith. Two things will determine the strength and "flavor" of your gifts:

1. The proportion of your faith determines how much grace you receive to operate in the gifts. In other words, the greater amount of faith you have inside you, the stronger the gifts will operate through you.

2. The type and level of grace that is resident in the one who is imparting the gift to you will determine what gift is given to you.

The following is an example of how grace and faith work: If we go to a soda fountain for a drink, the flavor of the drink is determined by the fountain—like the grace on a person's life who imparts the gift to us. The amount of the drink we are able to receive is determined by the size of the cup that we bring to the fountain—our faith.

It is important that we stay within the boundaries of our own faith and try not to copy another person's faith. We don't have to be profound to be powerful. Sometimes the simplest word touches people as deeply as something that seems heavy or profound.

> **You don't have to be profound to be powerful.**

Since we have gifts that differ according to the grace given to us, each of us is to exercise them accordingly: if prophecy, according to the proportion of his faith (Romans 12:6).

The gifts of the Holy Spirit are not awards! We cannot earn them. Because the gifts are not a mark of maturity, we do not have to wait for our lives to be in perfect order to receive them. Nonetheless, we are instructed to earnestly desire, which means "to passionately pursue them."

How the Gifts Grow

Jesus expressed His opinion about growing your gifts through the parable of the talents—if we *use* what we have received, more will be given to us. If we *do not use* what we have, even what we have will be taken away from us. This principle applies to every aspect of the Kingdom of God. If we want to receive a deeper level of prophetic revelation, then we must be faithful with the level of insight that we have now. Some people who have only received one talent spend all of their time trying to figure out why someone else received more, instead of stewarding what they have been given to attain more!

For it is just like a man about to go on a journey, who called his own slaves and entrusted his possessions to them. To one he gave five talents, to another, two, and to another, one, each according to his own ability; and he went on his journey. Immediately the one who had received the five talents went and traded with them, and gained five more talents. In the same manner the one who had received the two talents gained two more. But he who received the one talent went away, and dug a hole in the ground and hid his master's money.

Now after a long time the master of those slaves came and settled accounts with them. The one who had received the five talents came up and brought five more talents, saying, "Master, you entrusted five talents to me. See, I have gained five more talents." His master said to him, "Well done, good and faithful slave. You were faithful with a few things, I will put you in charge of many things; enter into the joy of your master."

Also the one who had received the two talents came up and said, "Master, you entrusted two talents to me. See, I have gained two more talents." His master said to him, "Well done, good and faithful slave. You were faithful with a few things, I will put you in charge of many things; enter into the joy of your master."

And the one also who had received the one talent came up and said, "Master, I knew you to be a hard man, reaping where you did not sow and gathering where you scattered no seed. And I was afraid, and went away and hid your talent in the ground. See, you have what is yours." But his master answered and said to him, "You wicked, lazy slave, you knew that I reap where I did not sow and gather where I scattered no seed. Then you ought to have put my money in the bank, and on my arrival I would have received my money back with interest. Therefore take away the talent from him, and give it to the one who has the ten talents" (Matthew 25:14-28).

The key to growing in your prophetic gift is *faithfulness.* Do you want to speak to thousands? Then prepare like you are speaking to thousands. Preach and teach like you are speaking to the masses, even if you have a youth group of five, or you are ministering on Sunday mornings at the hospital chapel. God looks at how we steward what we have before promoting us into what we desire. It is easy for us to look at people who seem to have "more talents" than we do and become jealous. We think we want what they have. Little do we know that we have what we have right now because it is what we can be safely entrusted with. If we had more, the more would destroy us instead of bless us. God is not looking for talent; He is looking for faithfulness. This is the key to growth and maturity in your prophetic gifting.

In First Timothy, Paul exhorts Timothy to "be absorbed in" and practice his spiritual gift so he would grow and set an example to others through his pursuit.

Do not neglect the spiritual gift within you, which was bestowed on you through prophetic utterance with the laying on of hands by the presbytery. Take pains with these things; be absorbed in them, so that your progress will be evident to all (1 Timothy 4:14-15).

In First Peter, we are exhorted to "employ" the gifts that have been given to us. If we don't become good stewards of the gifts that God has given us, He will give them to someone who will take responsibility for them. God has no unemployment insurance!

As each one has received a special gift, employ it in serving one another as good stewards of the manifold grace of God (1 Peter 4:10).

The Baptism of the Holy Spirit and Gifts

Jesus told His disciples to wait for the promise of the Father which, when received, would give them power from on high. The word power, in Greek, is the word dunamis, which is where we get the word dynamite. Therefore, the baptism in the Holy Spirit is the power behind the gifts. The gifts can be compared to the motor in a car, in the sense that the baptism in the Holy Spirit is the fuel!

But you will receive power when the Holy Spirit has come upon you; and you shall be My witnesses both in Jerusalem, and in all Judea and Samaria, and even to the remotest part of the earth (Acts 1:8).

Questions to Ponder

1. What is the most common way to receive the gifts of the Spirit?

2. What role does grace have for those who receive impartation from someone else?

3. What part does faith play in receiving the gifts of the Holy Spirit?

4. How do we grow stronger in the gifts that we already have?

Questions for Group Discussion

1. How do prophetic words equip people for battle?

2. First Corinthians 12:11 says that the Holy Spirit distributes His gifts as He wills. How does the Holy Spirit determine to whom He will give His gifts?

3. Are you able to grow in the gifts of the Holy Spirit? The prophetic?

4. What is the key to growing in a prophetic gift/ability?

5. What would be some problems of experiencing growth and increase in our prophetic giftings beyond our ability to manage them well?

6. Share about a time when you experienced growth in a gift in your life. How does this development happen? What was the catalyst? (Examples: impartation, prayer, etc.)

Life Application

Ask the Holy Spirit if you have been faithful with everything that He has given you. If you have not, ask Him for a plan for the areas where you have been afraid or apathetic. Remember that courage is fear that has said its prayers! It's been said that, "A coward dies a thousands deaths, but a brave person dies only once."

CHAPTER 7

Prophetic Etiquette

Most of us have experienced a right prophetic word in the wrong season or a wrong word in the right season! This chapter is all about how to speak the right word in the right season. Also discussed is what the proper delivery of a prophetic word should look like.

Your Prophetic Responsibility

Like apples of gold in settings of silver is a word spoken in right circumstances (Proverbs 25:11).

BACK IN THE OLD TESTAMENT, WHEN SAUL DISOBEYED THE LORD AND THE SPIRIT OF God departed from his life, he got in trouble. Unfortunately, his previous advisor and consultant—the prophet Samuel—was dead. So God was not speaking with him directly, and the prophet who had previously served as his earpiece to God was also dead (see 1 Samuel 28).

As a result, Saul travels to the witch of Endor and asks her to conjure up the spirit of Samuel. This practice of divination and necromancy was expressly forbidden. It was considered illegal. In fact, if Saul was caught, the penalty could have been as severe as being executed. Even though it was illegal, the witch still practiced divination and brought up the spirit of Samuel.

In Leviticus 19:31, the Lord expressly commands, *"Do not turn to mediums or necromancers; do not seek them out, and so make yourselves unclean by them: I am the Lord your God"* (ESV). God did not want Samuel to come up from the dead. Yet, the witch made something happen that God did not will or decree. This tells us that just because you can make something happen in the spirit world, does not validate that God actually wanted it to happen in the first place. Once He gives you authority to operate in the spirit realm, it is possible for you to do things that God does not necessarily want you to do.

Some would question, *Isn't God in control?* He is in charge, but He is not in control. If God was in absolute control of planet Earth, there would be no sin, no death, no sickness, no child abuse, no murder, no hatred, and the list continues. God is in charge of all things, but He has left you in control. In Psalm 115:16, we read that *"The heavens are the heavens of the Lord, but the earth He has given to the sons of men."* The earth realm is under the dominion and control of humankind.

This is a call for us to responsibly operate in prophetic ministry, recognizing that just because we *can* do something, does not mean God desires for us to do it. This is why we are establishing some guidelines for prophetic etiquette.

Many of us imagine something similar to the following example when we think of the prophetic ministry taking place in the church.

Many years ago when we first started attending a charismatic church, there was a woman who would abruptly stand up in the middle of the pastor's sermon. She would shake, tremble, and scream out a message in tongues nearly every Sunday. This was followed by an interpretation of equal volume, spoken in dramatic King James English.

In order to be effective, it is important for us to establish clear guidelines to proper prophetic ministry.

Guidelines to Proper Prophetic Ministry

The following guidelines are not meant to be laws, but merely intended to give some "banks to the river." Without banks, the river becomes a flood. In a flood, the water typically does more damage than good.

Every culture has its own unique flavor and style. It is essential, however, to realize that it is not our culture or style that makes a word prophetic. What makes a word prophetic is God speaking through someone.

Therefore, my brethren, desire earnestly to prophesy, and do not forbid to speak in tongues. But all things must be done properly and in an orderly manner (1 Corinthians 14:39-40).

An important key to proper prophetic ministry: the spirit of the prophet is subject to the prophet. This means that the Holy Spirit normally subjects Himself to the vessel He is using. People are not acting according to the standard set by Scripture when they say things such as, "God made me do that" or "The Spirit came upon me and I had to jump up and speak that out."

The spirits of prophets are subject to prophets (1 Corinthians 14:32).

The following examples illustrate times when it is inappropriate to give a prophetic word:

1. When we are angry or have strong, negative emotional feelings toward the person or people for whom we have a prophetic word.

2. When we use prophecy as a "platform" to validate our personal doctrines or belief system. Example: "I, the Lord, say to you tonight thou shall not go to movies!"

3. When we have no relationship or accountability to the person or group of people receiving our prophecy. It is important for prophetic people to have a sense of ownership of the people to whom they are ministering. Too often people have an "us" and "them" attitude toward the people they are ministering to. This is unhealthy and dishonoring.

Authority = Accountability + Responsibility + Accessibility

Delivery of the Prophetic Word

The following are practical guidelines for ministering and delivering prophetic words:

1. It is not necessary or recommended to use King James English when prophesying. King James English will not validate that what we are saying is from God. It simply means that we read the King James Version of the Bible. Incidentally, Jesus didn't speak King James English, nor did He sound like Shakespeare.

2. It is important that our demeanor matches that of the Holy Spirit's. In other words, it is just as important for us to correctly present the tone in which the Holy Spirit communicated the word to us as it is what He said. It is seldom necessary for us to yell—increasing the volume of our voice does not make the prophecy better. The tone of voice in which we say something to a person communicates just as much as the words themselves.

3. Love must be at the center of all we do in Christ. When we are ministering in the gifts of the Spirit, our motive must always be to bring out the best in people.

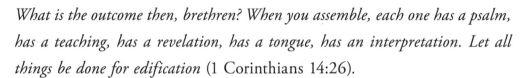

What is the outcome then, brethren? When you assemble, each one has a psalm, has a teaching, has a revelation, has a tongue, has an interpretation. Let all things be done for edification (1 Corinthians 14:26).

4. In a church service, the appropriate way to deliver a prophetic word is to submit it to the person or persons in charge of the service. At our church, prophecies are submitted to "gatekeepers" who are aware of what the Holy Spirit is doing with worship and what direction the sermon will take. These people are able to determine if a prophetic word will be fitting for a particular service. Remember, the goal of all prophecy is to present an accurate word in the right circumstances.

5. Phrases such as, "I the Lord say to you tonight," or "Thus saith the Lord," are seldom necessary. What makes a prophetic word the voice of God? God is the one who initiated it—not a person. When the prophecy is judged, it will be evident whether it was the Lord speaking or not.

Negative and/or Judgmental Words

The Bible is clear that life and death are in our words. When we give people negative words, we often release death over them. Our goal is to be part of a ministry that releases life and calls out the best in people.

Death and life are in the power of the tongue, and those who love it will eat its fruit (Proverbs 18:21).

Most of the time it is best to avoid giving negative or judgmental prophetic words.

Remember also that just because the word ends positively does not mean that it is an encouraging word. A good rule to follow: if you would not want to receive the word yourself, you should not give it to someone else.

A member of our prophetic team gave a pastor this word: "Like Job and his wife, you are about to endure a season of great loss; but in the end, the Lord will restore you to double, just like He did for Job."

Thankfully, this word was given to a mature pastor, otherwise the word could have been very damaging. The pastor did the right thing by bringing this word to our leadership and the team member was redirected in love.

Warning or Judgment Words

The following guidelines will help if you receive multiple warning or judgment words.

1. Ask yourself if negative words are common to you. If a high percentage of the prophetic revelation you receive is negative, you may be the problem.

2. Occasionally the Lord will warn of upcoming dangerous or negative situations. He informs us so we might pray for our or someone else's safety. Pray until the burden lifts.

3. Ask the Holy Spirit for a prophetic word that releases life into the situation. Remember, prophetic ministry releases grace for things to change. Prophesying the answer will uplift our spirits and come against the darkness that is threatening us.

4. If the warning persists, we should submit the word to our leadership. Once it is given over to them and we have relinquished ownership, they are now responsible. God will speak to them as we pray for Him to give them wisdom and guidance regarding the word.

Accountability

At times we may feel that the Lord has spoken to us about our own lives. In other words, we have prophesied over ourselves. As with any other prophetic word, it should be judged.

It is vitally important that we submit this word to those who have authority over us; just as we would if we had received it from someone else. This is especially true if the word involves direction.

When we articulate this type of word to leadership, we should not say, "The Lord *told* me to do this." That opening statement dramatically reduces their ability to give us their input. After all, who wants to argue with God?

When people go to leadership for counsel, and begin a conversation with, "The Lord *told* me to do this," in reality what they are often saying is, "I don't want your opinion; I just want your blessing for what I want to do."

I was once speaking with a pastor who shared that he had divorced his wife because "God told me to." He said that his son had a dream that he believed also validated his decision to leave his wife! While questioning him concerning his marriage, I asked him if his wife had committed adultery. "No," he replied, "nothing like that...she hated the ministry."

I thought he was going to fall out of his chair when I told him that God did *not* tell him to leave his wife.

Remember, we only have as much authority in God as we are willing to submit to.

We only have as much authority in God as we are willing to submit to.

If we only do what those in leadership over our lives tell us to do when we agree with them, that is not called submission, but rather "doing our own thing." We must invite leadership into our lives and learn to trust them more than we trust ourselves. Otherwise, if we ever become deceived in an area, the only way to find our way out of deception is to trust someone else more than ourselves. The very nature of deception is that we do not know we are deceived! If we know we are deceived, that is not called deception, but stupidity!

This doesn't mean that we should follow a leader whose life and ministry doesn't have good fruit. It also doesn't mean that we do something that the Bible clearly tells us is wrong just because a leader tells us to do it. We are to follow our leaders *as they follow Christ!*

Obey your leaders and submit to them, for they keep watch over your souls as those who will give an account. Let them do this with joy and not with grief, for this would be unprofitable for you (Hebrews 13:17).

Questions to Ponder

1. What are some reasons why it would be inappropriate to prophesy?

_____

_____

2. What are some things to watch for when delivering a prophetic word?

_____

_____

3. What is the proper procedure for delivering a prophetic word in a public service?

_____

_____

Questions for Group Discussion

1. Why do you think people sometimes yell or use King James English when delivering a prophetic word?

2. How do you determine the Holy Spirit's mood or attitude for the proper delivery of a prophetic word?

Life Application

Pray for the Holy Spirit to give you a prophetic word during a church service. Practice your prophetic protocol in delivering the word. Find the gatekeepers and give them the word that you believe the Lord gave you. Allow them to determine the authenticity and timing of the word. If you are given permission to deliver the word, be conscious of not just what to say but how to say it.

CHAPTER 8

False Prophets

Much has been written about false prophets. This chapter discusses the facts and fallacies surrounding them, and explains why a false prophet is not someone who gives a bad prophetic word but rather is someone who has an evil heart.

What Makes a False Prophet?

There are two types of false prophets. The first type is comprised of people who have invited a spirit of divination into their lives. The gift, which enables them to prophesy, comes from an evil spirit and has nothing to do with God. The gift is from hell and these people have let their hearts turn to evil. What is important to note: although the word is coming from a spirit of divination, it can still be accurate! Acts chapter 16 illustrates this principle through a false prophetess who has the right word, but the wrong spirit.

It happened that as we were going to the place of prayer, a slave-girl having a spirit of divination met us, who was bringing her masters much profit by fortune-telling. Following after Paul and us, she kept crying out, saying, "These men are bond-servants of the Most High God, who are proclaiming to you the way of salvation." She continued doing this for many days. But Paul was greatly annoyed, and turned and said to the spirit, "I command you in the name of Jesus Christ to come out of her!" And it came out at that very moment (Acts 16:16-18).

An example of this type of false prophet would be a psychic. Sometimes psychics can be very accurate with their predications, but they are not receiving their information from God. When one gives a prophetic word, it is being released and carried by the power of God. Operating in the prophetic means working in agreement with the angels of God. However, when a psychic or medium receives a prediction, this information is being delivered and ultimately fulfilled by demon spirits. A psychic, medium, or fortune-teller is operating out of a wrong heart and an evil spirit.

The second type of false prophet is the group of people who receive a call on their lives to be a prophet or prophetess from birth or after they receive Christ, yet they later fall away from God. Interestingly, in Romans 11:29, Paul states that the gifts and callings of God are irrevocable. Even if we fall away from God, we would still be able to operate in the gifts. However, this gift would not be in our control, but would be turned over to the hands of the evil one. In Numbers chapters 22 through 24, we read about a false prophet named Balaam. It is clear in the Scripture that Balaam is getting his prophetic revelation from God, but he is trying to use his gift to curse God's people so he can make money. Balaam has a gift from God but a heart from hell.

False Prophets' Characteristics

According to Matthew, false prophets have certain characteristics.

Beware of the false prophets, who come to you in sheep's clothing, but inwardly are ravenous wolves. You will know them by their fruits. Grapes are not gathered from thorn bushes nor figs from thistles, are they? So every good tree bears good fruit, but the bad tree bears bad fruit. A good tree cannot produce bad fruit, nor can a bad tree produce good fruit. Every tree that does not bear good fruit is cut down and thrown into the fire. So then, you will know them by their fruits.

Not everyone who says to Me, "Lord, Lord," will enter the kingdom of heaven, but he who does the will of My Father who is in heaven will enter. Many will say to Me on that day, "Lord, Lord, did we not prophesy in Your name, and in Your name cast out demons, and in Your name perform many miracles?" And then I will declare to them, "I never knew you; depart from Me, you who practice lawlessness."

Therefore everyone who hears these words of Mine and acts on them, may be compared to a wise man who built his house on the rock. And the rain fell, and the floods came, and the winds blew and slammed against that house; and yet it did not fall, for it had been founded on the rock. Everyone who hears these words of Mine and does not act on them, will be like a foolish man who built his house on the sand. The rain fell, and the floods came, and the winds blew and slammed against that house; and it fell—and great was its fall (Matthew 7:15-27).

The following are the common threads that run through the lives of the type of false prophet described in Matthew chapter 7:

1. False prophets appear to be good—like sheep—but are really like wolves. They are the enemy of the sheep. The bad fruit that they bear is not a false gift but rather an evil heart. Remember, these people will say to Jesus, "Did we not prophesy in Your name and cast out demons in Your name?" But He will say to them, "I never knew you." He calls them "lawless." It is interesting how Jesus defines "lawless" in Matthew chapter 7 in the description of the two different men building houses. He considered the one who heard His words but did not act on them to be lawless! Notice also that the Lord equates knowing Him with keeping His Word. No one can teach or instruct the false prophet, for he or she is lawless. It does not matter if these people are able to perform signs, wonders, and miracles; their true fruit is revealed in whether or not they know and obey God.

   If you love Me, you will keep My commandments (John 14:15).

2. False prophets have their belief system founded on a few pet Scriptures (sand) and not the whole counsel of God (the rock). False prophets take certain Scriptures out of context that advocate their own agenda. They find Scriptures, pull them out of a story or an idea, and create a new meaning.

3. False prophets have power. Unfortunately, their goal is to use their power to lead people to themselves, instead of to Christ. A false prophet makes his or herself the answer instead of God. Instead of showing the body of Christ how to hear God for themselves, false prophets act like they are the direct line to God. Sometimes this perspective is the result of immaturity and a lack of teaching on what the prophetic truly is. However, if they exhibit some of the other signs we have been reviewing, and very intentionally present their prophetic voices as the exclusive way that you can hear from God, they are treading on dangerous ground. Some people have a desire to be needed so badly that they lead people to themselves through their ministries instead of leading them to God.

For false Christs and false prophets will arise and will show great signs and wonders, so as to mislead, if possible, even the elect (Matthew 24:24).

It is important for us to be aware of this reality, as it is easy for people to assume that signs, wonders, and demonstrations of power confirm someone's legitimacy as an authentic prophet. They do not. At the same time, the Christian life cannot be devoted to hunting the false. This training is to build you up in what is true and authentic. When you are schooled in the authentic, you will easily be able to detect anything counterfeit or false.

Discerning the Difference

According to John, there is a way to discern the difference between a true prophet and a false prophet. In the end, it is all about the heart. What distinguishes a false prophet from a true prophet is the heart. It is not signs and wonders. It is not even the accuracy of a prophetic word. Remember, there are false prophets who give accurate words, and then there are also true prophets who occasionally make mistakes.

Christians can be deceived by the devil.

In the Book of First John, he gives us guidelines. The first verse of the text warns Christians to not become false prophets by believing the wrong spirit. This caution is sobering. Many Christians do not believe that evil spirits can influence them. One of the greatest deceptions in the church today is the idea that Christians cannot be deceived by the devil. The following Scripture passage clearly dispels that myth.

Beloved, do not believe every spirit, but test the spirits to see whether they are from God, because many false prophets have gone out into the world. By this you know the Spirit of God: every spirit that confesses that Jesus Christ has come in the flesh is from God; and every spirit that does not confess Jesus is not from God; this is the spirit of the antichrist, of which you have heard that it is coming, and now it is already in the world (1 John 4:1-3).

Five Tests of a True Prophet

1. False prophets do not believe in the redemptive work of the Son of God.

One thing to note is that false prophets are antichrist in nature. They are not anti-Jesus. The word Christ, or *Christos,* means "the anointed one." The anointing is always related to the power of God. Beware of people who try to tell you that Jesus doesn't do miracles anymore. This is not about some doctrine of miracles, signs, and wonders; it is about the livingness of Jesus. When we focus more on what we think Jesus does not do, we are presenting an inaccurate representation of who He is. This is dangerous, since Scripture tells us *"Jesus Christ is the same yesterday and today and forever"* (Heb. 13:8). According to Paul in Second Corinthians chapter 11, there is another "Jesus" who is not the Christ (anointed one). Again, the Jesus we serve was anointed yesterday, is anointed today, and will be anointed forever!

You are from God, little children, and have overcome them; because greater is He who is in you than he who is in the world. They are from the world; therefore they speak as from the world, and the world listens to them. We are from God; he who knows God listens to us; he who is not from God does not listen to us. By this we know the spirit of truth and the spirit of error (1 John 4:4-6).

2. False prophets do not like to listen to anyone; in their own minds, God tells them everything.

False prophets are hyper-spiritual in their conversations and begin most of their statements with, "The Lord said to me…" or "God told me…." I have found over the years that this is just a rather spiritual way of saying, "I don't want your input!" They are not under any authority but their own. How can you argue with someone who is basically telling you, "God told me this, and that's settled. Final. Period." You can't. Even if they are wrong or slightly misguided, they are convinced that they are correct, and by using that language, they are telling you—*I don't want your input, leadership, or guidance; I want you to bless what I want.*

Submission to God should be seen in the visible realm. Someone might say, "I am submitted to God," but when it comes to appropriately yielding to authority, he or she might resist. If we claim to follow Jesus, but do not follow the people He put in authority—for our benefit—we are doing ourselves a disservice. Remember, authority is not about restraining; it is about empowering. That said, there are many times in our lives when we need another voice to give us guidance, direction, and maturity-producing discipline. When we are resistant toward God-instituted authority—established to bring out the best in us and help us develop into maturity—we rob ourselves of growth opportunity and deny ourselves of the fruitfulness that the Holy Spirit wants to release through our lives.

Beloved, let us love one another, for love is from God; and everyone who loves is born of God and knows God. The one who does not love does not know God, for God is love. By this the love of God was manifested in us, that God has sent His only begotten Son into the world so that we might live through Him. In this is love, not that we loved God, but that He loved us and sent His Son to be the propitiation for our sins. Beloved, if God so loved us, we also ought to love one another. No one has seen God at any time; if we love one another, God abides in us, and His love is perfected in us. By this we know that we abide in Him and He in us, because He has given us of His Spirit. We have seen and testify that the Father has sent the Son to be the Savior of the world. Whoever confesses that Jesus is the Son of God, God abides in him, and he in God. We have come to know and have believed the love which God has for us. God is love, and the one who abides in love abides in God, and God abides in him. By this, love is perfected with us, so that we may have confidence in the day of judgment; because as He is, so also are we in this world (1 John 4:7-17).

False prophets think that when you correct them, you are persecuting them. They will try to cite things like, "You know, they persecuted the prophets of old." For one, they have nothing in common with the prophets of old, because we are under the New Covenant now. There are no more Old Covenant prophetic voices, so the comparison immediately falls apart. They will take different Scriptures out of context, about the ways that people—especially the kings—treated the prophets of old. This is what they perceive you are doing. Their argument not only falls apart (because they should not compare themselves to the prophets of old), but they are blatantly rejecting the words of Paul, *"and the spirits of prophets are subject to prophets"* (1 Cor. 14:32). The Amplified Bible expounds on this perfectly, saying that the spirits of the prophets are *"subject to being silenced as may be necessary."* In other words, they must be willing to receive correction, whether they are delivering a message in tongues, or sharing a prophetic word.

3. False prophets are not motivated by love but are motivated by a need to be noticed. The central theme of all ministries must be the love of God. We must ask ourselves: Am I in

the ministry for the purpose of bringing out the best in people? Do I have the kind of love that covers a multitude of sins?

> *We love, because He first loved us. If someone says, "I love God," and hates his brother, he is a liar; for the one who does not love his brother whom he has seen, cannot love God whom he has not seen. And this commandment we have from Him, that the one who loves God should love his brother also* (1 John 4:19-21).

4. False prophets commonly use fear to motivate people.

"Doom and gloom" tend to be the main thrusts of the false prophets' message. They also say things like, "God showed me something about you, but I can't tell you." This kind of statement breeds insecurity in people. False prophets revel in thinking that they "have something on you" that you don't know about!

> *There is no fear in love; but perfect love casts out fear, because fear involves punishment, and the one who fears is not perfected in love* (1 John 4:18).

Love is the central theme of the Gospel. If I am a prophet, or operating in prophetic ministry, and I don't have love defining everything I say and do, I have literally lost the entire point of the Gospel. This is one of the most distinguishing marks of a false prophet—one whose ministry is without love. Yes, we will make mistakes, mess up, and fail. This is expected. Again, there is a major difference between ones who are a work in progress, and ones who refuse to make progress because they assume the work is perfect. False prophets assume that they are a finished work. This is why they refuse direction and reject constructive criticism.

When love is at the core, humility always follows—even in the process of making mistakes and growing.

When love is at the core, humility always follows.

5. False prophets are not in covenant relationship with the Body of Christ.

I have yet to observe a false prophet who has a healthy relationship with the local body they attend. Many do not even attend church at all. They wander from place to place looking for people who will listen to them. Often, their goal is to gain a following, stealing people from "the flock." While such people tend to stir up dissension in local churches, this goes beyond that. It is one thing to change churches; false prophets, however, seduce people to the point of leaving the overarching community of believers. False prophets do have followings and fan bases. Just because someone has many people flocking around their ministry does not mean they are genuine prophetic voices. Because false prophets are not in covenant relationships with the Body of Christ, they recruit others out of church community to join their ranks in the spiritual wilderness.

The word covenant means that we are not in a relationship for what we can get from people but rather for what we can give. Covenant relationships are costly. Jesus, in John 15:13, says, *"Greater love has no one than this, that one lay down his life for his friends."*

Leading People Out of Prophetic Deception

Confronting those who believe they are true prophets, but are not, can be a rather difficult situation. Most false prophets have been abused by authority much of their lives and therefore do not trust anyone. Fear is the number one reason why people become hyper-spiritual, and it results in religious deception. To make matters worse, many false prophets have a martyr's complex. The more they are confronted about their weirdness, the more validated they feel. They interpret attempts at correcting them as persecution that proves they are "standing for God" and against the unrighteous religious system! They say things like, "I don't believe in organized religion," when the real problem is that they don't like boundaries. Remember, Jesus calls them "lawless." Lawless people are those who want to live outside of authority.

So how can they be helped? First of all, the leaders of the flock must not be afraid to confront these people even though they may appear to know more than the leadership and may be intimidating. Remember, "All that wickedness needs to prosper is for righteous men to do nothing." It is also important to not react but instead respond to these people; otherwise, the cure can be worse than the disease. People like this are accustomed to criticism and rejection, and will use it to validate their "ministry."

They can, however, be won over by true, godly discipline (not punishment). The difference between punishment and discipline: punishment says, "I will get even with you for the damage you have caused," but discipline says, "I love you too much to leave you broken."

The only hope for these people is when they begin to feel loved. As they experience the love of God, they can begin to trust the leadership to lead them out of their deception.

If they refuse to repent and submit to correction, they must be removed from fellowship; otherwise, they will lead others astray. As mentioned previously, the primary weakness of false prophets is that they draw people to themselves instead of to God. There is a very narrow window of time for leadership to deal with false prophets before they rally people to their defense against the leadership. They have an uncanny ability to attach themselves to the young or hurting sheep and are able to divide them from the flock. Finally, like wolves, they devour the sheep in deception.

Beware of false prophets!

Questions to Ponder

1. Name five things that distinguish a false prophet from a true prophet.

   _____

   _____

2. What is one of the main reasons why people become false prophets?

   _____

   _____

3. Why does opposing false prophets somehow seem to validate their ministry?

   _____

   _____

4. Is a person who gives inaccurate prophecies always a false prophet?

   _____

   _____

5. Can a person give accurate prophecies and still be a false prophet?

   _____

   _____

Questions for Group Discussion

1. Why is it important for believers to be able to recognize false prophets in their midst?

2. Explain why the demonstration of power and miracles is not a sign of a true prophet.

3. Why do you think that false prophets are so against submitting to authority?

4. In First John chapter 4, the beloved are warned not to become false prophets. How could someone who loves Jesus eventually fall into the category of a false prophet?

5. Do you see any of these tendencies in your own heart?

Life Application

Independence, fear, and pride all keep us from the deep relationships that we need with God and His people. It is so important that we have people in our lives in whom we trust more than we trust ourselves. Do you have a relationship with someone you would trust with your life? If that person told you that you have a problem, one that you don't see, would you believe that person even though it does not feel true? We need to build these kinds of relationships to keep us safe as we live on the edge. Go build a relationship with someone like that in authority.

CHAPTER 9

Practicing Prophecy

This chapter provides some practical lessons on various ways to practice the Gift of Prophecy and Words of Knowledge. It is only in practicing that your confidence grows and your accuracy increases.

Practicing the Gifts of the Spirit

Some Christians misunderstand the definition of practicing the gifts of the Holy Spirit. We are not practicing so that the Holy Spirit can improve His gifts, but rather we are practicing to improve our ability to flow with what the Holy Spirit is doing.

In the days of Samuel, Elijah, and Elisha, the sons of the prophets studied under the guidance of these prophets in what was probably a school of the prophets. Although the sons of the prophets were based out of Naioth in Ramah, they wandered throughout the wilderness practicing their prophecies while being mentored by these renowned prophets.

> *Then Saul sent messengers to take David, but when they saw the company of the prophets prophesying, with Samuel standing and presiding over them, the Spirit of God came upon the messengers of Saul; and they also prophesied* (1 Samuel 19:20).

Practicing the gifts of the Spirit should take place in an atmosphere of love and a culture of spiritual authority. Without being in submission to true spiritual authority, we are like a contractor who builds a skyscraper without a foundation. The first time the wind blows, it will fall to the ground.

No Pain—No Gain

In the Book of First Timothy, Paul exhorts Timothy to minister in his spiritual gift beyond his comfort zone. Anyone who has ever performed physical exercise knows that there is little profit to exercising until your body feels a degree of pain. Therefore, if we wake up the morning after exercising and we're not sore, we would realize that the exercise only maintained our current condition!

Reach beyond your comfort zone.

The same principle applies to our spiritual growth. If we only do what is comfortable for us, we will fail to grow. Whenever we are truly growing, there will always be an element of discomfort. You can look at it this way: the dogs of doom stand at the doors of destiny. In other words, the things you are afraid of often hold the greatest rewards.

Do not neglect the spiritual gift within you, which was bestowed on you through prophetic utterance with the laying on of hands by the presbytery. Take pains with these things; be absorbed in them, so that your progress will be evident to all (1 Timothy 4:14-15).

Put the Gift in the Fire

Paul, in Second Timothy 1:6, reminds Timothy to "*kindle afresh the gift of God.*" Looking to the Greek translation, this phrase signifies "putting the gift through the fire or joining the gift with fire." The next verse makes more sense now in this context: "*For God has not given us a spirit of fear, but of power and of love and of a sound mind*" (2 Tim. 1:7 NKJV).

Whenever we step out in faith, we must step over fear! Fear is the guard dog that is protecting the fortress of spiritual prosperity. When the dog starts barking, we can be sure that the treasure he is guarding is near. Most people do not allow their gifts to be forged in the fire of risk. The result: their gifts are weak and not tempered.

Therefore I remind you to stir up the gift of God which is in you through the laying on of my hands. For God has not given us a spirit of fear, but of power and of love and of a sound mind (2 Timothy 1:6-7 NKJV).

Suggestions for Practicing Prophecy

The following are practical suggestions for practicing the gifts of the Spirit.

1. Prophesy your day.

When you wake in the morning, pray and ask the Lord for information about something that will happen during your day. Write it down as clearly as you understand it. At the end of the day, check and see if the event that you prophesied to yourself happened. Also see how well you understood the specific details of the event(s).

2. Practice words of knowledge.

Go to a restaurant or public place of business and pray for the person who is providing a service for you. Ask the Lord for words of knowledge for the person. It is usually best if you do this when the person is not in your presence. Write down the words of knowledge on a piece of paper. Later you can "interview" the person concerning the words of knowledge you received.

For example, if you think the Lord showed you that the person you are receiving words for has three children; you can simply ask if he or she has any children. If the answer is yes, you can inquire how many, etc. When you are first learning, I would suggest you not tell the person that you have words of knowledge from God. In the beginning, this practice is more about you growing in your gift than about ministering. As your ability to hear the voice of the Holy Spirit improves, you will begin to step out in boldness and faith.

3. Team up with another person.

Enlist the help of a prayer partner. Pray for one another and ask the Lord for words of knowledge for each other. Take turns sharing what you believe God has shown you. Let the recipient judge the word you gave to him or her. Obviously this works best if both of you are trying to grow in your spiritual gifts. It is important in this exercise to be extremely truthful with one another so as to gain an honest assessment of how you are doing.

4. Words of knowledge for healing.

You can practice words of knowledge for healing in a group setting by simply praying and asking the Lord to show you anyone who is experiencing illness or pain. This will often come as a sensation in your body that directly coincides with the part of someone else's body that the Lord wants to heal. If it is appropriate in the meeting, ask the group if anyone has the specific problem in their body. Then afterward, you should pray for that person and experience the joy of seeing the Lord heal the person!

5. Prophesying as a group.

Another way to practice in a group setting is to choose one member of the group and have the others prophesy to that person. As the words are given, ask a member of the group to write them down. After an adequate number of prophetic words are given, ask the person who received the prophetic words to judge the words and give feedback to the group about the accuracy of the word.

6. Prophetic intercession.

Prophetic intercession is practiced as we pray. Often in prayer the Lord will give you insight into people's lives. Prophesy the answer to each of the issues that you see in the lives of these people and then ask the Lord to let your paths cross that day. You will be amazed at how many times the Lord will bring people to your mind to pray for—people you haven't seen in months, or even years. Most likely, you will soon hear from them.

Questions to Ponder

1. Name the greatest obstacle that we must overcome to see our gifts grow.

_____

_____

2. How can we tell when we are growing in our gifts?

_____

_____

3. Name three ways in which we can practice our spiritual gifts.

_____

_____

_____

Questions for Group Discussion

1. Share one experience that you had when you stepped over fear into faith. What did you learn from the experience?

2. What is your greatest fear when you consider walking in the fullness of your gifts?

3. What are you going to do about your fear?

4. Take this opportunity to practice what you just learned. Pick someone in the group to prophesy over, and then have the person judge the accuracy of the words he or she received.

Life Application

Create a plan to overcome your greatest fears to stepping out in your gifts. Then become accountable to someone to carry out your plan.

Epilogue

EACH AND EVERY DAY THE WORLD WAKES UP TO THE BAD NEWS OF A PLANET IN DECAY. Depression and death press into our minds and steal our courage. Even our homes that were once safe places for children to grow up in love have become, for many, battlefields where little ones must run for cover. Sticks and stones are breaking their bones and names are taking away their future.

Yet in all of this confusion, there is still a God who only rested one day. His creative proclamations that instilled life and goodness in the Book of Genesis perpetuate through His vessels even to this day. It is He who reigns supremely over all of His creation. He is not depressed, confused, afraid, or perplexed over the darkness of this planet. He speaks into those who are formless and void, and life is the result of His words!

I know a man who over 35 years ago had a nervous breakdown. The breakdown lasted for more than three and a half years. His hands trembled so violently that he could not even bring a glass of water to his lips without using both hands. He would sweat so profusely at night from fear and anxiety that his wife would have to get up in the middle of the night and change the soaking wet sheets. As time went on he began to lose his mind and many times a day he would envision himself murdering people—or worse. Demons visited and tormented him throughout the night.

Then one afternoon some friends persuaded him to attend a Christian retreat in the mountains. That day a prophet was speaking at the meeting. He called the young man out of the crowd and prophesied to him. He said, "The Lord has called you to be a pillar in the house of God. You shall be a teacher and a pastor to His people. Strength is in you!"

The war in that man's life was won that day. I know that man very well—I am that man!

Never underestimate the redemptive power of God's prophetic ministry. There are many people starving to know who they really are. You have the ability to alter the history of people who are lost and broken.

Don't disappoint them.

Personal Experience Journal

THE FORMS ON THE FOLLOWING PAGES WERE CREATED TO HELP YOU KEEP TRACK OF your dreams, visions, and prophecies. Recording your experiences will assist you in developing accountability that builds up your faith. These records may be used as learning and/or teaching tools similar to the films that athletes use of their previous games to improve their abilities. You may want to copy the pages and create a prophetic journal.

Let the journey begin!

Dreams and Visions

Date: _____

Dream or Vision Description:

_____

_____

_____

_____

_____

_____

_____

Interpretation:

_____

_____

_____

_____

_____

_____

_____

Application:

_____

_____

_____

_____

_____

_____

_____

Date of fulfillment: _____

Dreams and Visions

Date: _____

Dream or Vision Description:

_____

_____

_____

_____

_____

_____

_____

Interpretation:

_____

_____

_____

_____

_____

_____

_____

Application:

_____

_____

_____

_____

_____

_____

_____

Date of fulfillment: _____

Dreams and Visions

Date: _____

Dream or Vision Description:

_____

_____

_____

_____

_____

_____

_____

_____

Interpretation:

_____

_____

_____

_____

_____

_____

_____

Application:

_____

_____

_____

_____

_____

_____

_____

Date of fulfillment: _____

Dreams and Visions

Date: _____

Dream or Vision Description:

_____

_____

_____

_____

_____

_____

_____

Interpretation:

_____

_____

_____

_____

_____

_____

Application:

_____

_____

_____

_____

_____

_____

Date of fulfillment: _____

Dreams and Visions

Date: _____

Dream or Vision Description:

_____
_____
_____
_____
_____
_____
_____

Interpretation:

_____
_____
_____
_____
_____
_____
_____

Application:

_____
_____
_____
_____
_____
_____
_____

Date of fulfillment: _____

Dreams and Visions

Date: _____

Dream or Vision Description:

_____

_____

_____

_____

_____

_____

_____

Interpretation:

_____

_____

_____

_____

_____

_____

_____

Application:

_____

_____

_____

_____

_____

_____

_____

Date of fulfillment: _____

Dreams and Visions

Date: _____

Dream or Vision Description:

_____

_____

_____

_____

_____

_____

_____

Interpretation:

_____

_____

_____

_____

_____

_____

_____

Application:

_____

_____

_____

_____

_____

_____

_____

Date of fulfillment: _____

Prophetic Words

Date: _____

_____

_____

_____

_____

_____

_____

_____

_____

Word given by: _____ Word given to: _____

Date: _____

_____

_____

_____

_____

_____

_____

_____

_____

Word given by: _____ Word given to: _____

Date: _____

_____

_____

_____

_____

_____

_____

_____

_____

Word given by: _____ Word given to: _____

Prophetic Words

Date: _____

_____

_____

_____

_____

_____

_____

_____

Word given by: _____ Word given to: _____

Date: _____

_____

_____

_____

_____

_____

_____

_____

Word given by: _____ Word given to: _____

Date: _____

_____

_____

_____

_____

_____

_____

_____

Word given by: _____ Word given to: _____

Prophetic Words

Date: _____

_____

_____

_____

_____

_____

_____

_____

Word given by: _____ Word given to: _____

Date: _____

_____

_____

_____

_____

_____

_____

_____

Word given by: _____ Word given to: _____

Date: _____

_____

_____

_____

_____

_____

_____

_____

Word given by: _____ Word given to: _____

Prophetic Words

Date: _____

_____

_____

_____

_____

_____

_____

_____

_____

Word given by: _____ Word given to: _____

Date: _____

_____

_____

_____

_____

_____

_____

_____

_____

Word given by: _____ Word given to: _____

Date: _____

_____

_____

_____

_____

_____

_____

_____

_____

Word given by: _____ Word given to: _____

Prophetic Words

Date: _____

_____

_____

_____

_____

_____

_____

_____

Word given by: _____ Word given to: _____

Date: _____

_____

_____

_____

_____

_____

_____

_____

Word given by: _____ Word given to: _____

Date: _____

_____

_____

_____

_____

_____

_____

_____

Word given by: _____ Word given to: _____

About Kris Vallotton

Kris Vallotton is the senior associate leader of Bethel Church in Redding California and has served on Bill Johnson's apostolic team for more than thirty-four years. He has written nine books, including the bestselling Supernatural Ways of Royalty and Spirit Wars. Kris's revelatory insight and humorous delivery make him a much sought after international conference speaker.

Kris and Kathy Vallotton have been happily married since 1975. They have four children and eight grandchildren.